Best Easy Day Hikes
Cincinnati

Help Us Keep This Guide Up to Date

Every effort has been made by the author and editors to make this guide as accurate and useful as possible. However, many things can change after a guide is published—trails are rerouted, regulations change, facilities come under new management, etc.

We would appreciate hearing from you concerning your experiences with this guide and how you feel it could be improved and kept up to date. While we may not be able to respond to all comments and suggestions, we'll take them to heart and we'll also make certain to share them with the author. Please send your comments and suggestions to the following address:

GPP
Reader Response/Editorial Department
P.O. Box 480
Guilford, CT 06437

Or you may e-mail us at:

editorial@GlobePequot.com

Thanks for your input, and happy trails!

Best Easy Day Hikes Series

Best Easy Day Hikes
Cincinnati

Johnny Molloy

FALCONGUIDES

GUILFORD, CONNECTICUT
HELENA, MONTANA
AN IMPRINT OF GLOBE PEQUOT PRESS

FALCONGUIDES®

Copyright © 2011 by Morris Book Publishing, LLC

FalconGuides is an imprint of Globe Pequot Press.

Falcon, FalconGuides, and Outfit Your Mind are registered trademarks
of Morris Book Publishing, LLC.

TOPO! Explorer software and SuperQuad source maps courtesy of
National Geographic Maps. For information about TOPO! Explorer,
TOPO!, and Nat Geo Maps products, go to www.topo.com or www
.natgeomaps.com.

Project editor: David Legere
Layout artist: Kevin Mak
Maps created by Hartdale Maps © Morris Book Publishing, LLC.

Library of Congress Cataloging-in-Publication Data is available on file.

ISBN 978-0-7627-6356-6

Printed in the United States of America

10 9 8 7 6 5 4 3 2 1

Contents

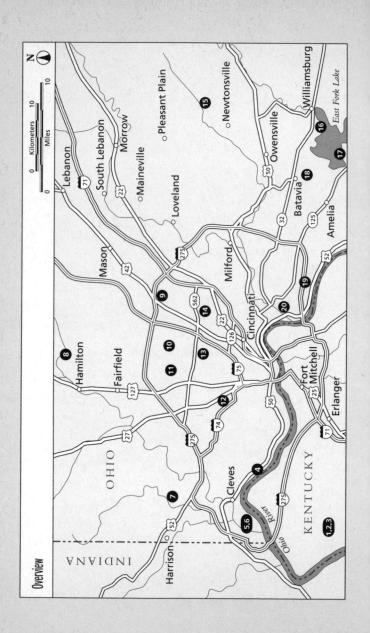
Overview

Acknowledgments

Thanks to all the people who helped me with this book, primarily the people at Falcon, including Scott Adams, Jess Haberman, and David Legere. Thanks to Pam Morgan, Kent Roller, and Heather Morgan for their help. Thanks to Lafuma for their warm sleeping bags and good-fitting packs, to DeLorme for their accurate global positioning systems, and to Merrell for quality hiking shoes and boots. Also, thanks to all the park personnel who answered my tireless questions while trying to manage these jewels of greater Cincinnati. The biggest thanks go to the trail builders and hikers of the area, for without y'all there wouldn't be trails in the first place.

Introduction

The astonishing view stretched to the horizon. I sat on a bench, surveying the landmarks below—the Great Miami River where it flowed into the mighty Ohio River, the green hills of Kentucky and Indiana beyond. Shawnee Lookout was but one of many gorgeous and historic destinations in this book. I mentally reflected on other destinations, recounting all the scenic hikes of greater Cincinnati. Along the Ohio River corridor, one hike travels beside the big water while availing views near and far. Another river hike has still more views and old-growth forest. To the south, two hikes explore important state nature preserves, where big trees stand centuries in the making. Another hike roams creek bottoms with even bigger trees, a place of stunning scenery. Withrow Nature Preserve displays yet another great view of the Ohio River from atop impressive bluffs. Forest areas to the north offer loops traveling hills, streams, and ponds in a biologically rich array of flora and fauna.

One hike wanders along the historic Miami-Erie Canal while also diving through a waterfall-filled canyon. Developed parks combine recreational trails with paths voyaging through protected natural areas. Yet another hike visits developed gardens and beyond, into pond, meadow, and creek wetlands and through restored prairies. East Fork State Park has its own jewels. The Fern Hill Trail presents a loop that surmounts hilly terrain cut by rocky streams in deep hollows. Another hike roams along the East Fork Lake and through diverse flatwoods. Other watery venues include Sycamore Park, where the hike cruises by river rapids and pools bordered with wildflower-rich bottoms. In-town

Cincinnati avails its own destinations. Mount Airy Forest, one of Cincinnati's first parks, delivers a woodsy circuit that includes a trip up the famed Stone Steps. Caldwell Nature Preserve has big trees, views, and clear creeks. The Creek Trail at French Park features everywhere-you-look beauty as French Creek cascades over layer after layer of limestone.

With this book in hand and willing feet, you can explore the greater Cincinnati region. No matter where you go, the trails in this book will enhance your outdoor experience and leave you appreciating the natural splendors of the Tri-state. Enjoy.

The Nature of Greater Cincinnati

Cincinnati's hiking grounds range from single-track wooded trails along rivers to hilly paths high atop bluffs and astride lakes to flat park strolls. Hikes in this guide cover the gamut. While by definition a best easy day hike is not strenuous and generally poses little danger to the traveler, knowing a few details about the nature of greater Cincinnati will enhance your explorations.

Weather

Cincinnati certainly experiences all four seasons. Summer can be warm, with occasional downright hot spells. Morning hikers can avoid heat and the common afternoon thunderstorms. Hiking increases when the first northerly fronts of fall sweep cool clear air across the Ohio Valley. Crisp mornings give way to warm afternoons. Fall is drier than summer. Winter will bring frigid subfreezing days, chilling rains, and snows. However, a brisk hiking pace will keep you warm. Each cold month has a few days of mild weather. Make the most of them. Spring will be more variable. A warm day can be followed by a cold one. Extensive spring rains bring regrowth but also keep hikers indoors. But any avid hiker will find more good hiking days than they will have time to hike in spring and every other season.

Critters

Cincinnati trail treaders will encounter mostly benign creatures on these trails, such as deer, squirrels, rabbits, wild turkeys, and a variety of songbirds. More rarely seen (during the daylight hours especially) are coyotes, raccoons, and opossums. Deer in some of the parks are remarkably tame and may linger on or close to the trail as you approach. If you feel uncomfortable when encountering any critter, keep your distance and they will generally keep theirs.

Be Prepared

Hiking in greater Cincinnati is generally safe. Still, hikers should be prepared, whether they are out for a short stroll at Winton Woods Park or venturing into secluded sections of the East Fork State Park. Some specific advice:

- Know the basics of first aid, including how to treat bleeding, bites and stings, and fractures, strains, or sprains. Pack a first-aid kit on each excursion.

- Familiarize yourself with the symptoms of heat exhaustion and heat stroke. Heat exhaustion symptoms include heavy sweating, muscle cramps, headache, dizziness, and fainting. Should you or any of your hiking party exhibit any of these symptoms, cool the victim down immediately by rehydrating and getting him or her to an air-conditioned location. Cold showers also help reduce body temperature. Heat stroke is much more serious: The victim may lose consciousness and the skin is hot and dry to the touch. In this event, call 911 immediately.

- Regardless of the weather, your body needs a lot of water while hiking. A full 32-ounce bottle is the minimum for these short hikes, but more is always better. Bring a full water bottle, whether water is available along the trail or not.

- Don't drink from streams, rivers, creeks, or lakes without treating or filtering the water first. Waterways and water bodies may host a variety of contaminants, including giardia, which can cause serious intestinal unrest.

- Prepare for extremes of both heat and cold by dressing in layers.

- Carry a backpack in which you can store extra clothing, ample drinking water and food, and whatever goodies, like guidebooks, cameras, and binoculars, you might want. Consider bringing a GPS with tracking capabilities.

- Most Cincinnati trails have cell phone coverage, but you can never be absolutely sure until you are on location. Bring your device, but make sure you've turned it off or got it on the vibrate setting while hiking. Nothing like a "wake the dead"–loud ring to startle every creature, including fellow hikers.

- Keep children under careful watch. Trails travel along many rivers, streams, ponds, and lakes, most of which are not recommended for swimming. Hazards along some of the trails include poison ivy, uneven footing, and steep drop-offs; make sure children don't stray from the designated route. Children should carry a plastic whistle; if they become lost, they should stay in one place and blow the whistle to summon help.

Leave No Trace

Trails in Cincinnati and neighboring communities are well used year-round. We, as trail users, must be especially vigilant to make sure our passage leaves no lasting mark. Here are some basic guidelines for preserving trails in the region:

- Pack out all your own trash, including biodegradable items like orange peels. You might also pack out garbage left by less considerate hikers.

- Don't approach or feed any wild creatures—the ground squirrel eyeing your snack food is best able to survive if it remains self-reliant.

- Don't pick wildflowers or gather rocks, antlers, feathers, and other treasures along the trail. Removing these items will only take away from the next hiker's experience.

- Avoid damaging trailside soils and plants by remaining on the established route. This is also a good rule of thumb for avoiding poison ivy and other common regional trailside irritants.

- Be courteous by not making loud noises while hiking.

- Many of these trails are multiuse, which means you'll share them with other hikers, trail runners, mountain bikers, and equestrians. Familiarize yourself with the proper trail etiquette, yielding the trail when appropriate.

- Use outhouses at trailheads or along the trail.

Cincinnati Area Boundaries and Corridors

For the purposes of this guide, best easy day hikes are confined to a one-hour drive from downtown Cincinnati and are primarily in Hamilton and Clermont Counties, with one in Butler County. Three hikes are in Boone County, Kentucky.

A number of major interstates converge in Cincinnati. Directions to trailheads are given from these arteries. They include I-75, I-74, I-71, and I-275—the main loop around Cincinnati.

Land Management

The following government organizations manage most of the public lands described in this guide and can provide further information on these hikes and other trails in their service areas.

- Hamilton County Park District, 10245 Winton Rd., Cincinnati, OH 45231; (513) 521-7275; www.greatparks.org
- Cincinnati Parks, 950 Eden Park Dr., Cincinnati, OH 45202; (513) 352-4080; www.cincyparks.com
- Ohio State Parks, 2045 Morse Rd., C-3, Columbus, OH 43229; (614) 265-6561; www.dnr.state.oh.us/

How to Use This Guide

This guide is designed to be simple and easy to use. Each hike is described with a map and summary information that delivers the trail's vital statistics including length, difficulty, fees and permits, park hours, canine compatibility, and trail contacts. Directions to the trailhead are also provided, along with a general description of what you'll see along the way. A detailed route finder (Miles and Directions) sets forth mileages between significant landmarks along the trail.

Hike Selection

This guide describes trails that are accessible to every hiker, whether visiting from out of town or someone lucky enough to live in greater Cincinnati. The hikes are no longer than 5 miles round-trip, and most are considerably shorter. They range in difficulty from flat excursions perfect for a family outing to more challenging hilly treks. While these trails are among the best, keep in mind that nearby trails, often in the same park or preserve, may offer options better suited to your needs. I've sought to space hikes throughout the greater Cincinnati region, so wherever your starting point, you'll find a great easy day hike nearby.

Difficulty Ratings

These are all easy hikes, but easy is a relative term. To aid in the selection of a hike that suits particular needs and abilities, each is rated easy, moderate, or more challenging. Bear in mind that even most challenging routes can be made easy by hiking within your limits and taking rests when you need them.

- **Easy** hikes are generally short and flat, taking no longer than an hour to complete.
- **Moderate** hikes involve increased distance and relatively mild changes in elevation and will take one to two hours to complete.
- **More challenging** hikes feature some steep stretches, greater distances, and generally take longer than two hours to complete.

These are completely subjective ratings—consider that what you think is easy is entirely dependent on your level of fitness and the adequacy of your gear (primarily shoes). If you are hiking with a group, you should select a hike with a rating that's appropriate for the least fit and prepared in your party.

Approximate hiking times are based on the assumption that on flat ground, most walkers average 2 miles per hour. Adjust that rate by the steepness of the terrain and your level of fitness (subtract time if you're an aerobic animal and add time if you're hiking with kids), and you have a ballpark hiking duration. Be sure to add more time if you plan to picnic or take part in other activities like birding or photography.

Trail Finder

Best Hikes for Lake Lovers

Best Hikes for Children

Best Hikes for Dogs

Best Hikes for Great Views

Best Hikes for Solitude

Best Hikes for River and Stream Lovers

Best Hikes for Nature Lovers

Map Legend

≡≡75≡≡	Interstate Highway
≡50≡	U.S. Highway
≡52≡	State Highway
═══	Local Road
▬▬▬▬	Featured Trail
- - - - -	Trail
├──┼──┼──┤	Railroad
— · · — · · —	State Line
∿	River or Stream
▰	Body of Water
⇗	Boat Ramp
⌣	Bridge
■	Building/Point of Interest
▲	Campground
�!	Gate
▲	Mountain/Peak
🅿	Parking
⊞	Picnic Area
⊞	Restroom
o⌐	Spring
○	Town
❶⑦	Trailhead
◈	Viewpoint/Overlook
❷	Visitor/Information Center
⋟	Waterfall

1 Boone County Cliffs State Nature Preserve

Owned by The Nature Conservancy, this seventy-four-acre tract preserves glacially carved hills in Kentucky's Boone County. The hike travels along a tributary of Middle Creek and through hilly woodland containing old-growth trees. The cliffs harbor some of the most biologically diverse flora and fauna in northern Kentucky and are an important bird habitat.

Distance: 1.7-mile loop
Approximate hiking time: 1.0 to 1.5 hours
Difficulty: Moderate, but has elevation changes
Trail surface: Natural surfaces
Best season: Year-round
Other trail users: None
Canine compatibility: Dogs not permitted

Fees and permits: No fees or permits required
Schedule: Sunrise to sunset
Maps: Trailhead kiosk map; USGS Rising Sun
Trail contacts: Kentucky State Nature Preserves Commission, 801 Schenkel Lane, Frankfort, KY 40601; (502) 573-2886; www.naturepreserves.ky.gov

Finding the trailhead: From exit 181 on I-75 south of downtown Cincinnati, take KY 18 west for 10.6 miles to Middle Creek Road. Turn left onto Middle Creek Road and follow it 1.7 miles to the trailhead on your left. GPS: N38° 59' 35.59", W84° 47' 4.66"

The Hike

This gem of a wooded hilly tract not only preserves unique plants and animals of the area while harboring old-growth forest but is also simply a great hiking destination. A primitive loop trail circles a centerpiece stream, highlighted by the 20 x 40-foot cliffs found between the tops of ridges and the stream below. Anywhere you have cliffs you are going to have elevation changes, and the single-track path takes you on a ride that includes nearly 300 feet in elevation undulations, so be prepared for some vertical variation. The Nature Conservancy originally made their first preservation purchase of forty-two acres in 1974, then expanded it in 1990. It is not only the sloping terrain that creates the special plant habitat but also the soils and cliffs composed of glacial gravel outwash, rare in these parts. Birds and birders flock to this destination—over ninety species of avian life have been recorded, including resident and migratory species. The deep hollow offers copious wildflowers in spring, and the wide diversity of trees makes for a colorful autumn display.

The trail is mostly easy to follow. Wooden posts keep you apprised of your position. Brush can crowd the track in summer, but the primitive condition of the path adds a wilderness aspect to the trek. Contemplation benches make for desirous stopping spots.

A natural surface trail leads you up a tributary of Middle Creek. The down cutting of the tributary created the cliffs of the preserve. Maple, white oak, basswood, and beech tower over the trail. Sycamores crowd the clear stream below, which gurgles over rocks and sand. The hollow tightens, and soon you are in uplands, taking a short spur to an overlook that allows views into the creek below. The modest cliffs lie at your feet. Ahead you will pass through an impressive beech grove. Unfortunately, the smooth gray bark has proven too tempting for passersby, who carve into the giants. Other tall trees rise from the ridgetop.

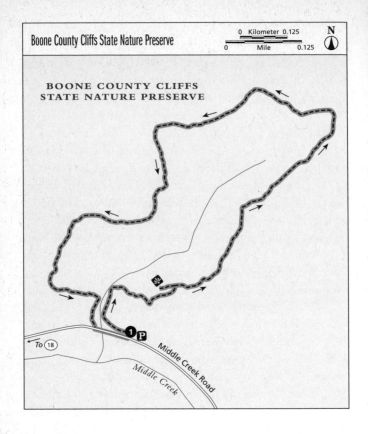

0   Kilometer 0.125

N

0   Mile   0.125

BOONE COUNTY CLIFFS
STATE NATURE PRESERVE

To (18)

Middle Creek Road

Middle Creek

The loop continues circling around the unnamed tributary, availing views into fern-filled hollows below and views of other big trees, especially cherry. Also look for previous signs of human habitation, such as old fencelines and faint roadbeds, especially visible in leafless winter. The loop finally meets the creek, which is home to the dusky salamander. The amphibian needs exceptionally clean water, another reason for the preserve, the first Nature Conservancy property purchased in Kentucky. Enjoy listening to the singing stream shoals as they tumble toward Middle Creek. A very short road walk delivers you back to the trailhead.

Miles and Directions

0.0 Pass the trailside kiosk, which contains a map on its back side. Travel uphill, coming alongside a rocky tributary of Middle Creek.

0.1 Turn away from the stream and ascend sharply up a hill. Briefly level off at a contemplation bench then resume the climb, breaking through a cliff line.

0.3 Reach a trail intersection. Head left and walk a short distance along a ridge to a view of the watershed below. Your overlook is encircled by a cliff line. Backtrack to main loop.

0.5 Enter the head of a cove, passing beneath some huge beech trees. A contemplation bench allows you to look around for the entirety of them and to absorb the natural splendor of old-growth forest.

0.7 The trail turns sharply west. The major climb of nearly 300 feet is over as you tramp along the ridgetops.

1.1 The loop turns southwesterly at a ridgetop contemplation bench. The hollow to your left drops off sharply.

1.4 The downgrade steepens as it makes for the unnamed tributary. Watch your footing among the rocks and tree roots.

1.6 Come alongside the stream, continuing downhill past minor cascades. Emerge on Middle Creek Road within sight of the trailhead. Turn left onto Middle Creek Road.

1.7 Reach the trailhead, completing the hike.

2 Middle Creek Park Loop

This Boone County park trail system will surprise. Your hike traverses bottomlands where ancient and enormous sycamores curve skyward in incredible arcing beauty. Middle Creek is an alluring stream in its own right. Leave the bottomlands to roam among deeply wooded hills draining into Middle Creek. Along the way you will visit an old chimney from a forgotten cabin before dropping back to Middle Creek and completing the loop. Other shorter trails bisect this circuit in case you want to alter your hike.

Distance: 3.0-mile loop
Approximate hiking time: 2.0 to 2.5 hours
Difficulty: More challenging due to elevation changes
Trail surface: Natural surfaces
Best season: Year-round, fall will have drier trails
Other trail users: Equestrians
Canine compatibility: Leashed dogs permitted

Fees and permits: No fees or permits required
Schedule: Sunrise to sunset
Maps: Middle Creek Park; USGS Rising Sun
Trail contacts: Boone County Parks and Recreation, 35501 Middle Creek Rd., Burlington, KY 41005; (859) 334-2117; www .boonecountyky.org/parks

Finding the trailhead: From exit 181 on I-75 south of downtown Cincinnati, take KY 18 west for 11.0 miles, passing the historic Dinsmore Homestead on your right just before making the left turn into the Middle Creek Park entrance road. The trailhead is a short piece down the entrance road. GPS: N38° 59' 54.0", W84° 48' 51.9"

The Hike

Middle Creek Park is a pure nature park overlain with trails. It was once part of the greater Dinsmore Homestead, a historic preserved farm located just across KY 18, the two-lane road leading from nearby Burlington to the park. Being a part of the homestead property allowed for the preservation of the massive sycamores located along Middle Creek. One double-trunked sycamore may have more wood mass than any other tree for miles. A total of 6 trail miles lace the 230-acre park. However, hiking here has a downside: The trail system is shared with equestrians. In places, especially along the Middle Creek bottoms, the paths can be muddy, but you can usually work around these squishy spots. To offset the negative possibilities, avoid hiking here after rainy periods. Another good way to avoid the mud is to hike here from late summer through fall, when the trails will be at their driest. Mud aside, the big trees are worth a visit any time of year, except during deer hunting season, when the park is closed. Please consult Kentucky Department of Fish and Wildlife Resources at www.fw.ky.gov for the exact dates, which are generally in late fall.

The trail system is well signed and marked, but some user-created equestrian paths may briefly confuse. This hike follows Trail #1 most of the way, as it makes the widest loop through the forest. The trailhead offers numerous shaded picnic tables and a restroom for your convenience.

The hike shortly reaches Middle Creek, bridging the clear, gravelly stream bordered by mud banks. You then cruise through bottomland floodplain forest highlighted by massive sycamores, making graceful skyward arcs. Watch your footing, avoiding mud spots. It isn't long before the first junction with other interior paths. Gain glimpses of Middle Creek along the way. You won't miss the double-trunked sycamore before climbing from the creek, gaining 200 feet in elevation.

Loop your way along ridges, under regal oaks and arrow-straight tulip trees. Reach an odd stone chimney perched on a narrow ridge. The hike then descends toward Middle Creek, tracing an old roadbed back to the bridge, which carries you back to the trailhead.

Miles and Directions

- **0.0** With your back to KY 18, take the wide path, Trail #1, heading southeast past shaded picnic tables. The other trail leaving the parking area is for equestrians. Drop off a hill to make the Middle Creek bottoms. Turn left, cruising upstream along Middle Creek.

- **0.1** The Equestrian Access Trail comes in from your left. Keep straight.

- **0.2** Make the substantial bridge over Middle Creek just after an access leaves left for Dinsmore Homestead. At the Middle Creek bridge, look for a nearby massive sycamore with a trunk so large it would take several people together to stretch their arms around it. Stay left at a four-way trail junction along the creek on Trail #1, keeping in bottoms. Maple ash, buckeye, sycamore, and tulip trees shade the trail.

- **0.6** Intersect Trail #2. It leaves right and uphill, away from the bottoms.

- **0.8** Reach the huge double-trunked sycamore to the left of the trail. Its sheer mass is amazing. Trail #1 curves right, tracing Middle Creek.

- **0.9** Trail #4 leaves right. Stay with Trail #1. It keeps straight, then begins ascending away from Middle Creek.

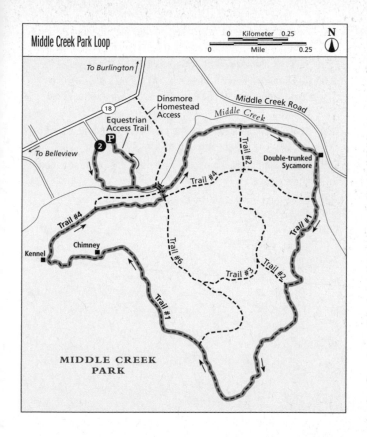

Middle Creek Park Loop

0 Kilometer 0.25

0 Mile 0.25

N

To Burlington

18

To Belleview

Dinsmore Homestead Access

Equestrian Access Trail

P 2

Middle Creek Road

Middle Creek

Trail #2

Double-trunked Sycamore

Trail #4

Trail #4

Trail #1

Kennel

Chimney

Trail #6

Trail #3

Trail #2

Trail #1

MIDDLE CREEK PARK

1.2 Top out on a ridge and reach a trail junction. Trail #2 and #3 leave right. Stay straight with Trail #1, undulating in hollow and hill.

1.8 Trail #6 leaves right. Keep straight on Trail #1, making a brief descent.

2.1 Pass a giant oak to the left of trail.

2.2 Reach a stone chimney of an old hunt cabin. Sharply descend among rock outcrops and through a cedar grove.

2.4 Emerge onto a field near a kennel. Turn right here, reentering woods. Trace a shaded roadbed back toward the bridge over Middle Creek. Watch for user-created spur trails.

2.6 Reach a trail junction. Here, Trail #1 drops left for Middle Creek. Keep forward, now on Trail #4, staying with the old roadbed.

2.8 Reach a trail junction near the Middle Creek Bridge. Turn left, bridging the stream, and backtrack.

2.9 Reach the Equestrian Access Trail. Take this path for added new mileage.

3.0 Make the trailhead, completing the hike.

3 Dinsmore Woods State Nature Preserve

This protected parcel of northern Kentucky lies within the historic land tract of the Dinsmore Homestead, an early-1800s preserved living history farm that once covered 700 acres. Old-growth woodland can be found on glacially carved, steeply sloped hills. The hike first passes the homestead and an adjacent cemetery before climbing 250 feet to a ridge. The loop meanders through the 107-acre preserve before completing the circuit. Consider pairing a hike with a visit to Dinsmore, open select days April through November.

Distance: 1.8-mile lollipop
Approximate hiking time: 1.5 to 2.5 hours
Difficulty: More challenging due to elevation changes
Trail surface: Natural surfaces
Best season: Fall through spring
Other trail users: None
Canine compatibility: Leashed dogs permitted

Fees and permits: No fees or permits required
Schedule: Sunrise to sunset
Maps: USGS Rising Sun, Lawrenceburg
Trail contacts: Kentucky State Nature Preserves Commission, 801 Schenkel Lane, Frankfort, KY 40601; (502) 573-2886; www.naturepreserves.ky.gov

Finding the trailhead: From exit 181 on I-75 south of downtown Cincinnati, take KY 18 west for 11.0 miles, passing the historic Dinsmore Homestead on your right, just before making the left turn onto the Middle Creek Park entrance road. The trailhead is a short piece down the entrance road. This is also the Middle Creek Park trailhead. The trail at Dinsmore Woods starts immediately across the road entrance to Middle Creek Park, on the north side of KY 18. GPS: N38° 59' 54.0", W84° 48' 51.9"

The Hike

Dinsmore Woods State Nature Preserve is part of a connected greater wild tract that includes 230-acre Middle Creek Park and the 30 acres surrounding Dinsmore Homestead. Known for its old-growth woodland, most notably big white oak and red oak, sugar maple, and ash trees, the preserve was initially established in 1990. But judging by the size and age of the trees, the preserve was much longer in the making. The whole shooting match was set in motion in 1839 when James Dinsmore bought 700 acres of land, then built and completed the Boone County house by 1842. Dinsmore raised a family with his wife, Martha, including one daughter, Julia, who lived on the property until age ninety-three. The homestead was purchased by a foundation and is now operated as a historic home where you can tour the house and grounds. For tour fees, information, and operating hours, visit www.dinsmorefarm.org. They also offer educational programs for children, Scouts, and adults and rent the facility for luncheons, weddings, and more.

In 1985 a wild parcel of the former farm was donated to The Nature Conservancy and later became part of the Kentucky state nature preserve system. The trail system was then constructed. Some hikers begin the loop at the homestead, and that is why the trail is more heavily used after you meet the spur trail coming from it. Pass several big trees before beginning the loop, which makes its way to a ridgetop. The primitive track can be faint with a few fallen trees across it, though trail signs and metal markers reassure hikers. In summer, brush grows thick astride the path, leaving fall through spring the ideal period for your first hike here. In winter

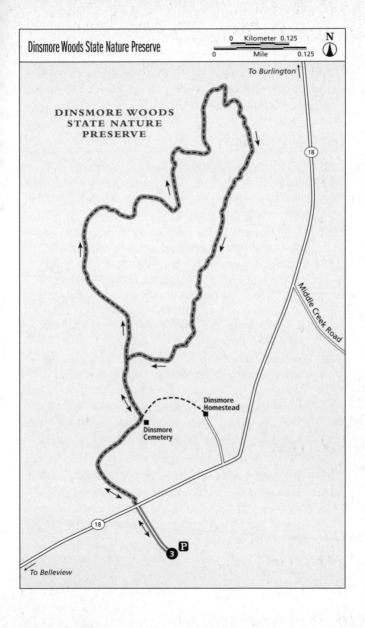

Dinsmore Woods State Nature Preserve

0   Kilometer   0.125
0   Mile   0.125

N

To Burlington

DINSMORE WOODS
STATE NATURE
PRESERVE

18

Middle Creek Road

Dinsmore
Homestead

Dinsmore
Cemetery

18

3 P

To Belleview

you will gain easterly views across Middle Creek valley atop the ridge. Your descent is on a side slope and can be challenging. An old roadbed offers easier trekking. Complete the loop then backtrack to the parking area, or cruise the grounds of the Dinsmore Homestead.

Miles and Directions

0.0 From the Middle Creek Park trailhead, backtrack to KY 18, cross KY 18, and enter Dinsmore Woods. Follow a faint track to the right then work left, north, to a hilltop, where the trail leads toward the homestead.

0.3 Reach the Dinsmore Cemetery and a grove of endangered buffalo running clover. Hand-laid stone walls topped with decorative ironwork encircle the family graves. A spur trail leads right, downhill to the Dinsmore Homestead. This hike leads left back into full-fledged woodland and uphill, passing the first of many huge oaks on trail left. The track shows more signs of use here. Reach the loop portion of the hike. Stay left with the loop.

0.6 Top out after climbing nearly 300 feet. Grab some air while traveling northerly on the ridgetop. The path also dips into drainages on the east side of the ridge.

0.9 The trail reaches its most northerly point on the ridge. Begin curving south and downhill on an extremely declivitous slope. Watch your step. Eventually join an old roadbed and level off.

1.3 Cross a pair of rocky drainages, then unexpectedly ascend.

1.5 Complete the loop portion of the hike. Turn left and backtrack toward the trailhead, passing the Dinsmore Cemetery. Consider going left at the cemetery and checking out the Dinsmore Homestead.

1.8 Arrive back at the Middle Creek Park parking area, completing the hike.

4 Fernbank Park Hike

Take a walk along the banks of the big Ohio River at this nicely redone Hamilton County Park. First, you will roam level riverside woodlands through a natural area on the Sycamore Trail. That loop will return you to the trailhead, where a more civilized asphalt track circles the park proper, once part of an Army Corps of Engineers lock managing area. Attractive and historic shelters, buildings, and picnic areas make including a picnic in your park visit a no-brainer.

Distance: 2.3-mile double loop
Approximate hiking time: 1.5 to 2.0 hours
Difficulty: Easy
Trail surface: Natural surfaces, concrete, and asphalt
Best season: Year-round
Other trail users: Bicyclists on paved trail
Canine compatibility: Leashed dogs permitted

Fees and permits: No fees or permits required
Schedule: Sunrise to sunset
Maps: Fernbank Park; USGS Burlington
Trail contacts: Hamilton County Park District, 10245 Winton Rd., Cincinnati, OH 45231; (513) 521-7275; www.greatparks.org

Finding the trailhead: From exit 1D on I-75 in downtown Cincinnati, take US 50 west/OH 264 west for 11.6 miles to Thornton Road. Turn left onto Thornton Road, cross the railroad tracks, and turn left again to enter the park. Follow the main park road to its end, parking near the Lee Shelter. The Sycamore Trail starts in the southeast corner of a nearby circular drive. GPS: N39° 7' 4.46", W84° 41' 59.74"

The Hike

Fernbank Park has undergone many incarnations. Located along the banks of the Ohio River near the community of Sayler Park, it is now a fine preserve managed by Hamilton County. It was wilderness before Cincinnati came to be. Later it was sporadically tilled and was also a steamboat landing. Early in the twentieth century, the land contained a complex of structures built by the U.S. Army Corps of Engineers. They operated Lock and Dam # 37 on the river, in use from 1910 to 1963. Lee Park and River Park bordered the lock. These lands were stitched together to form fifty-eight-acre Fernbank Park.

Last century's lock and dam system on the Ohio aided river commerce. It took several men to maintain each lock on the river. Here, four homes were built for employees as well as a main building, a powerhouse for operating the lock gates, a water tower, and an administrative office. The administrative office still stands and is now known as Fernbank Lodge. Hamilton County utilized the on-site park structures and integrated them into the current park plan, which also included the asphalt loop, popular with runners and walkers who live nearby. They also kept part of the park in a primitive state, and this is where the Sycamore Trail meanders.

In winter you'll be gaining immediate views of the river, but in summer the forest will have a thick junglesque appearance. Locust, sycamore, and ash tower overhead. User-created spur trails lead toward the river. Be careful using these trails, as they can be quite slippery and downright muddy in some places. If you want to access the water, wait until you are on the asphalt trail.

The hiking is easy on the flat Sycamore Trail. Repose benches are scattered along the way. A quiet seat with your ears open will reveal the area as a travel corridor: on either side of this park are a barge-filled river, a railroad, and highway. This narrow park is no wilderness today but is a slice of a getaway in an area where moving from point A to point B is the name of the game. Even we as hikers are moving.

After completing the Sycamore Trail, the hike picks up a partly shaded asphalt path. The groomed aspect contrasts with the uncultivated woods astride the Sycamore Trail. But the manicured section also opens views of the river and surrounding parkland where other visitors will be walking, bicycling, picnicking, playing with their kids, or simply relaxing as they overlook the Ohio and the state of Kentucky. The trail here is developed more as a promenade with shade trees and attractive iron benches. Ahead stands nicely preserved holdover structures from the Army Corps of Engineers days, as well as an old concrete boat ramp that leads to the river's edge. This is your chance to go down and see the river up close. Continue looping around park facilities, including a playground and the river shelter. Make sure to explore the full park, bridging a tributary of the Ohio River before tracing the trail back to where you started.

Miles and Directions

0.0 From the southeast end of the circular drive near the Lee Shelter, pick up the Sycamore Trail as it leaves the developed part of the park and enters dense woods along the Ohio River. Travel southeasterly on an elevated berm above the river.

0.2 Reach the loop portion of the Sycamore Trail. Turn right here, passing spur trails that lead to the water.

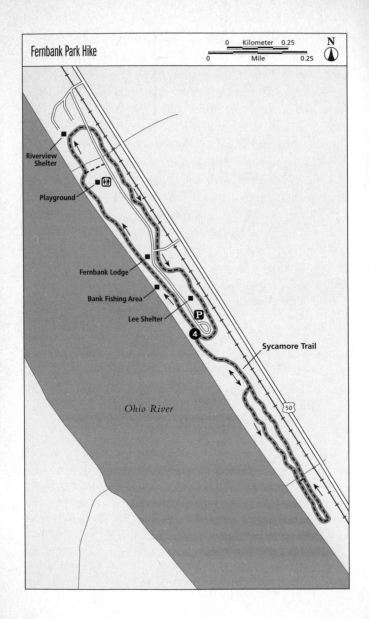

Fernbank Park Hike

| 0 | Kilometer | 0.25 |
| 0 | Mile | 0.25 |

N

Riverview
Shelter

Playground

Fernbank Lodge

Bank Fishing Area

Lee Shelter

P

4

Sycamore Trail

Ohio River

50

0.4 Negotiate a few wooden steps going into what is left of Doublelick Run, the only vertical variation of the hike. Just ahead, a grassy spur trail leads left to shortcut the loop.

0.5 The Sycamore Trail curves back toward the main part of the park. The CSX Railroad is to your right, through the trees.

0.9 Complete the Sycamore Trail loop. Backtrack through woods.

1.1 Join the asphalt path traveling along the Ohio River.

1.2 Pass the bank fishing area on your left, then the Fernbank Lodge. Continue along the river, passing the park playground.

1.5 Turn left onto a concrete path, bridging a stream flowing into the Ohio. Shortly pass the Riverview Shelter.

1.7 Reach the redone concession stand from when the area was River Park. Cross the main park road and begin looping back toward the trailhead.

2.0 Cross a now-gated alternate park entrance.

2.2 Pass behind Lee Shelter, then curve back toward the parking area.

2.3 Complete the hike.

5 Shawnee Lookout

This hike explores extensive Paleo-Indian earthworks located high on a ridge dividing the Great Miami River and Ohio River. Controversy swirls as to the purpose of the earthworks, whether they are military (a fort), ceremonial (a religious site), or practical (an irrigation system for a farm village). This hike explores the area William Henry Harrison dubbed "Fort Miami" and also travels to a stellar vista where you can see the confluence of the rivers and three states at once—Ohio, Kentucky, and Indiana.

Distance: 1.4-mile loop

Approximate hiking time: 1.0 to 1.5 hours

Difficulty: Easy

Trail surface: Pea gravel

Best season: Year-round, fall and winter are best

Other trail users: None

Canine compatibility: Leashed dogs permitted

Fees and permits: Parking fee required

Schedule: Sunrise to sunset

Maps: Shawnee Lookout Park; USGS Lawrenceburg

Trail contacts: Hamilton County Park District, 10245 Winton Rd., Cincinnati, OH 45231; (513) 521-7275; www.greatparks.org

Finding the trailhead: From exit 21 on I-275 west of downtown Cincinnati, take Kilby Road south for 1.0 mile to US 50. Turn right onto US 50 west and follow it 1.7 miles to Lawrenceburg Road. Turn left onto Lawrenceburg Road and follow it 0.7 mile, crossing the Great Miami River. Reach a T intersection. Turn right, still on Lawrenceburg Road, and follow it 0.5 mile to Shawnee Lookout Park, on your left. Turn into the park and climb away from the ranger station, tracing the main park road to dead-end at the trailhead after 1.9 miles. GPS: N39° 7' 14.13", W84° 48' 31.07"

The Hike

No matter what archaeological theory to which you sub-
scribe for Fort Miami, you will be firmly convinced this
is one of the most scenic hikes in greater Cincinnati. The
well-maintained gravel path, officially called the Miami
Fort Trail, takes you uphill into thousands of years of Ohio
Indian life. Trailside information signage helps explain the
human and natural history of this strategic location. If you
are ever going to read trailside interpretive information,
do it here and now, even if it is not entirely correct and
espouses now controversial theories as to the existence of
the fort.

In summer, the ridgetop forest will be quite thick with
cherry, locust, and walnut, under which grows copious
small pawpaw trees, partially obscuring the earthworks and
surrounding views of the Great Miami River and the Ohio
River. If you come when the leaves are off the trees, you
will be rewarded with not only better river views but also
a better lay of the earthworks, which by any measure were
done with nearly incomprehensible amounts of human
labor, perhaps over many centuries.

The trail leads to the main earthworks, where you
make a loop. This area has been visited by local residents,
surveyed by archaeologists, and theorized over by nearly
everyone. Mounds, earthen walls, and scooped-out areas are
visible. Most of the earthworks are now covered with trees,
though some parts have been kept open. The latest theories
center on the earthworks being part of a grand water management project. It's easy to see from here that the rivers
are hundreds of feet down and area springs simply couldn't
meet the water demand of the tribes, therefore they created

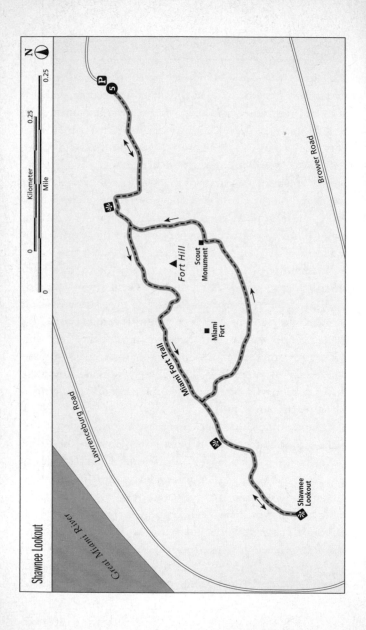

Shawnee Lookout

Great Miami River

Lawrenceburg Road

Brower Road

Miami Fort Trail

Fort Hill

Miami Fort

Scout Monument

Shawnee Lookout

N

Kilometer

Mile

0   0.25

0   0.25

ponds and runoff-catching areas with canals to enhance the agricultural possibilities of this protected, defensible area on high.

The trail undulates along a ridgeline dropping toward the Great Miami River. After leaving the main earthworks, it continues westerly toward the point of the ridge and views that await you. The first vista overlooks a large wetland of the Great Miami River. The park protects over 250 acres of seasonally flooded riparian habitat along with nearly a thousand additional acres of wetlands below. These wetlands provide habitat for area wildlife as well as migratory waterfowl that use the Ohio River flyway. The best view of all lies at trail's end—Shawnee Lookout. Take a seat on the bench and scan westward. The Ohio River and its wooded ramparts are easily identifiable. Kentucky stands on its south bank. Below, you can see the Great Miami River meandering to add its flow to the Ohio. An imaginary north–south line divides the Buckeye State from Indiana. It runs just below Shawnee Lookout. Anything you see west of the Great Miami River will be the Hoosier State. Given the lay of the land, it is easy to see this area as a highly defensible position.

Your return trip takes you by more earthworks. Imagine all the work in moving the soil by hand! By this point you are probably coming down on one side or another of the theories as to why these earthworks were established. No matter your theory, we can all agree that Shawnee Lookout is a great park and hiking destination.

Miles and Directions

0.0 Begin the Miami Fort Trail, ascending from the auto turnaround and parking area at road's end.

0.2 Reach the loop portion of the hike and the main earthworks, after passing a view of the Great Miami River.

0.5 Reach a trail intersection. The loop turns back and circles the main earthworks. However, keep straight, heading westerly to Shawnee Lookout.

0.6 Pass a vista overlooking wetlands of the Great Miami River.

0.7 Reach the Shawnee Lookout, where views of three states open. Backtrack to the main loop.

0.9 Turn right and resume the main loop, curving around the primary concentration of earthworks and bridging a couple of wet weather streams.

1.1 Pass a monument commemorating one of the founders of the Boy Scouts.

1.2 Complete the loop. Begin backtracking toward the trailhead.

1.4 Reach the trailhead, completing the hike.

6 Little Turtle/Blue Jacket Double Loop

This double loop hike travels two trails emanating from the same trailhead. Shawnee Lookout Park is the site of this trek, where superlatively maintained paths lead you first to bluffs rising 200 feet above the Ohio River. Enjoy watery views from cleared vistas. The second hike leads toward the Great Miami River. This one is more of a simple forest walk, though it does offer one view of the Great Miami. The clean, well-kept park is alluring itself and has picnic areas and shelters, as well as a historic cabin and schoolhouse.

Distance: 3.2-mile double loop
Approximate hiking time: 2.0 to 2.5 hours
Difficulty: Moderate
Trail surface: Pea gravel
Best season: Year-round
Other trail users: None
Canine compatibility: Leashed dogs permitted

Fees and permits: Parking fee required
Schedule: Sunrise to sunset
Maps: Shawnee Lookout Park; USGS Lawrenceburg, Hooven
Trail contacts: Hamilton County Park District, 10245 Winton Rd., Cincinnati, OH 45231; (513) 521-7275; www.greatparks.org

Finding the trailhead: From exit 21 on I-275 west of downtown Cincinnati, take Kilby Road south 1.0 mile to US 50. Turn right onto US 50 west and follow it 1.7 miles to Lawrenceburg Road. Turn left onto Lawrenceburg Road and follow it 0.7 mile, crossing the Great Miami River. Reach a T intersection. Turn right, still on Lawrenceburg Road, and follow it 0.5 mile to Shawnee Lookout Park, on your left. Turn into the park and climb away from the ranger station, tracing the main park road, passing the visitor center and golf course to reach the trailhead after 0.7 mile. Parking is to the right of the road. GPS: N39° 7' 30.5", W84° 47' 27.8"

The Hike

Your first trail of the hike, the Little Turtle Trail, was the first hiking trail constructed at Shawnee Lookout Park. The pea gravel path, named for a Miami Indian chief, meanders through level woods of white ash, locust, hackberry, and more. If you think you are walking in a circle, you are ¾ right. The trail curves three fourths of the way around a field for reasons known only to the trail builders. Pass a deer exclosure—an area where deer are excluded to test their effect on the park flora upon which they browse. The exclosure creates a test plot to see if they are altering the vegetational patterns of Shawnee Lookout.

Eventually, the path breaks northeasterly to reach the loop portion of the hike. An extraordinary number of cherry trees flank the nearly level trail. Vines curl and twist among the trees, while trailside brush grows nearly impenetrable during the warm season. Interpretive signage adds an educational aspect to the trek. Soon you will come along a lofty bluff towering over the Ohio River. The trail travels the bluff edge and reaches a cleared vista, where you can peer into the Bluegrass State. Hickories and oaks predominate on this drier ridgeline. Grab one last view before turning away from the river then passing an Indian burial mound. Before you know it you are back at the trailhead.

The second path, the Blue Jacket Trail, also named for a chief, starts on the same side of the road where you park. If you forgot something, now is a good time to get it. Otherwise, pick up the wooded path as it travels northwesterly away from the road and toward the Great Miami River. Pass under a couple of power lines before curving along a bluffline of the Great Miami. Shortly reach a cleared overlook of the Great Miami River valley, where views stretch well into Indiana. The path leaves the bluff and makes its way through pawpaw woods before opening to a power line and completing the loop. It is but a short walk to finish the hike.

Miles and Directions

0.0 From the parking area on the west side of the main park road, cross the park road toward the playground. Near the playground note the circular stone pit now covered in sand. Its purpose is unclear, but it is surmised that this was once an ice storage pit used by settlers who lived where this park now stands. Look for the Little Turtle Trail sign at a point where the grass ends and woodland begins.

0.3 Pass a fenced deer exclosure on your right.

0.4 Reach the loop portion of the hike and a four-way junction (the grassy track heading left accesses a trail shelter). Turn right here, toward the Ohio River.

0.7 Come along the bluff line above the Ohio River. The trail turns northeasterly, paralleling the bluff.

0.8 Reach a cleared view of the Ohio River Valley.

1.0 Pass a second cleared river view. The path then turns away from the bluff line and ascends.

1.1 Pass beside an aboriginal Ohioan burial mound. Paleo-Indian habitation has been documented at least 2,000 years back.

1.4 Bridge a streambed by culvert.

1.6 Complete the Little Turtle loop; backtrack to the parking area.

2.0 Reach the trailhead. Cross the main park road and pick up the Blue Jacket Trail. Slightly descend into thick woodland.

2.2 Pass under a power line. Reenter woods.

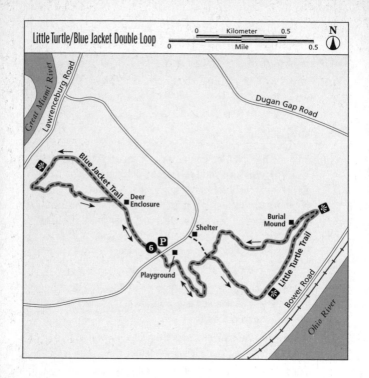

Little Turtle/Blue Jacket Double Loop

2.3 Reach the loop portion of the Blue Jacket Trail. Keep straight, passing under a second power line.

2.6 Reach a cleared view of the Great Miami River Valley and points west into Indiana. Soon turn away from the bluff.

2.9 Complete the loop, and backtrack toward the trailhead.

3.2 Arrive back at the trailhead parking area.

7 Loops of Miami Whitewater Forest

Make three loops on three different trails starting from the same trailhead at this 4,300-acre county forest that includes not only hiking trails but also camping, fishing, boating, and more. Your hikes travel through hilly terrain with frequent elevation changes, adding to the hiking challenge. However, you don't have to take the entire trek; simply pick one or two of the loop trails included and save the last one for another day. What value—three hikes in one destination! Small lakes and wet-weather streams add a watery aspect to the wooded setting.

Distance: 3.8-mile triple loop
Approximate hiking time: 2.0 to 3.0 hours
Difficulty: More challenging due to numerous hills
Trail surface: Natural surfaces and gravel
Best season: Year-round
Other trail users: None
Canine compatibility: Leashed dogs permitted

Fees and permits: Parking fee required
Schedule: Sunrise to sunset
Maps: Miami Whitewater Forest; USGS Shandon, Addyston, Harrison, Hooven
Trail contacts: Hamilton County Park District, 10245 Winton Rd., Cincinnati, OH 45231; (513) 521-7275; www.greatparks.org

Finding the trailhead: From exit 3 on I-74 west of downtown Cincinnati near the Indiana state line, take Dry Fork Road north for 0.9 mile to turn right onto West Road. Follow West Road for 0.2 mile to Timberlakes Drive. Turn left onto Timberlakes Drive and follow it 1.0 mile to the Timberlakes shelter and trailhead with a large parking area on your left. GPS: N39° 15' 1.76", W84° 44' 54.47"

The Hike

Each of the three trails is classified as a nature trail by the Hamilton County parks department. And I agree, they offer quiet walks in woodlands. For better or worse, you will be returning to the trailhead between each of the three hikes. The trailhead offers a picnic area, a covered shelter, restrooms, and water. Your first trail, Timberlakes Trail, is the most water oriented. It passes by a small dammed pond and comes near the big body of water at this park—Miami Whitewater Forest Lake.

It is but a short downhill jaunt on the Timberlakes Trail through hickory-oak woods to reach the dammed pond. The trail actually crosses the dam, and you can gain views of the impoundment from there. The hike then takes you up to a ridgeline where the trail offers easy walking. It comes near the access road for Miami Whitewater Forest Lake before running parallel to that impoundment. Return to the ridgeline, traveling south in rich deciduous woods before looping down to the small pond you were at earlier.

Next up is the Oakleaf Trail. It loops by the aforementioned pond, as well as a different smaller pond, with cattails and duck moss during the warm season. A boardwalk leads along the perimeter of the wetland and a steep hill with beech and buckeye. The Oakleaf Trail roller-coasters through a hickory–oak–maple complex. A highlight of this trail is the spur to a pond overlook with a contemplation bench perfect for relaxation. A solid climb brings you back to the parking area for your third trail.

Pick up the Badlands Trail across Timberlakes Drive. The Badlands Trail is named for the unusual land formations, which I attribute to erosion from poor land practices in days gone by. Sometimes it's hard to look at a forest and think of it as once being cleared, but this was likely pasture or farmland that lost topsoil following storms. You will be traveling into drainages that flow during winter, early spring, and following heavy rains. Bridges span some of the rocky streambeds. These drainages divide wooded hills over which you ramble. If you are tiring, take the Badlands Trail shortcut. Otherwise, stick with the whole loop and earn the complete 3.8 miles of the hike.

Miles and Directions

0.0 From the lower end of the parking area, away from the restrooms and Timberlakes Shelter, pick up the Timberlakes Trail heading easterly and downhill.

0.2 Cross the dam of a pond and reach the loop portion of the Timberlakes Trail. Turn left, northwesterly, following the dammed tributary.

0.4 Reach a mini-loop of the Timberlakes Trail on top of a ridge. Saunter north on a level wooded track toward Harbor Ridge Drive.

0.6 Come near Harbor Ridge Drive before turning back south, hiking a hill above Miami Whitewater Forest Lake.

0.7 Complete the mini-loop and proceed southerly along the ridge.

1.1 Come near the dammed pond.

1.4 Reach the trailhead after crossing back over the pond dam. Stay left and pick up the Oakleaf Trail, which starts near the Timberlakes Shelter.

1.5 Bridge the dam of a smaller pond. Begin the loop of the Oakleaf Trail, passing over a boardwalk.

1.9 Reach the spur trail leading to a contemplation bench at the edge of a pond. The Oakleaf Trail then rises to the trailhead after completing its loop.

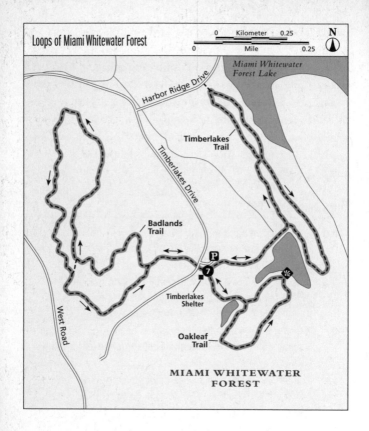

Loops of Miami Whitewater Forest

0 Kilometer 0.25
0 Mile 0.25

N

Miami Whitewater Forest Lake

Harbor Ridge Drive

Timberlakes Trail

Timberlakes Drive

Badlands Trail

West Road

P 7

Timberlakes Shelter

Oakleaf Trail

MIAMI WHITEWATER FOREST

2.2 Begin the Badlands Trail on the west side of West Road. Descend on wooden steps to a wooded hollow and the loop portion of this trail. Begin a pattern of dipping into drainages and climbing ridges.

2.3 Stay right at the loop of the Badlands Trail.

2.6 A shortcut leads left to bisect the loop portion of the Badlands Trail. Stay right with the longer circuit.

3.0 Curve back south on a hill well above Dry Fork Whitewater River.

3.4 Pass the other end of the Badlands Trail shortcut.

3.7 Complete the loop of the Badlands Trail.

3.8 Arrive back at the trailhead after finishing all three loops of Miami Whitewater Forest.

8 Rentschler Forest Hike

This Butler County park offers you a chance to hike along the historic Miami–Erie Canal, which once connected the Ohio River to Lake Erie, and also to see some waterfalls. The 400-acre preserve offers a half-mile frontage along the Great Miami River as well as nearly 6 miles of hiking divided over five trails. This hike takes the Pumpkin Vine Trail through woodland, passing relics of former dwellings before descending to reach the historic canal. Parallel the canal awhile then return to the trailhead. Next, pick up the Cascades Trail. It takes you along a rocky stream that drops steeply toward the Great Miami River, passing a couple of waterfalls and other rocky shoals.

Distance: 1.9-mile double loop
Approximate hiking time: 1.0 to 2.0 hours
Difficulty: Moderate, but has hills
Trail surface: Natural surfaces
Best season: Year-round
Other trail users: None
Canine compatibility: Leashed dogs permitted

Fees and permits: Entrance fee required
Schedule: Sunrise to sunset
Maps: Rentschler Forest Preserve; USGS Hamilton, Trenton
Trail contacts: Metro Parks of Butler County, 2051 Timberman Rd., Hamilton, OH 45013; (513) 867-5835; www.butlercounty metroparks.org

Finding the trailhead: From exit 24 on I-75 north of downtown Cincinnati in Butler County, take OH 129, Veterans Highway, west for 7.0 miles to OH 4 Bypass. Take OH 4 Bypass north for 1.6 miles to a traffic light at OH 4, Hamilton-Middleton Road. Keep straight at the light, now on Indian Meadows Drive. Follow Indian Meadows just a short distance, then turn right at a stop, still on Indian Meadows Drive, to meet Reigart

Road. Turn left onto Reigart Road and follow it 0.6 mile into Rentschler Forest Preserve. In the park, head left, passing the entrance station, going to the road's end, parking near the Condo Shelter. GPS: N39° 25' 14.96", W84° 30' 19.60"

The Hike

The United States relied on canals before there were railroads and trucks for shipping. The state of Ohio invested heavily in a canal system to transport products from source to market and people from place to place. Parts of the canals were hand dug. Each canal was generally 4 feet deep and bordered by berms 2 feet above the water level. One berm contained a 10-foot-wide towpath. Horses and mules pulled the boats along the canal. It took over twenty years to complete the Miami-Erie Canal. The canal system included 105 locks to raise and lower the boats along the waterway, which climbed as high as 500 feet above the Ohio River and nearly 400 feet above Lake Erie on its cross-Ohio journey. Railroads rendered canals obsolete, and the canal was entirely defunct by 1929.

Before you reach the canal on the Pumpkin Vine Trail, it will take you through young woods of cedar and walnut past some forgotten homesites with trees growing among the walls, old farm implements, and even a well. Soon you are at the canal. Your easterly journey takes you past old artifacts and of course along the grown-in canal bed to your left. All too soon leave the canal and climb back toward the parking area. The Pumpkin Vine Trail takes you back to the parking area.

The Cascades Trail leaves from a nearby parking area, within sight. This path cruises woods near houses then circles into a limestone rock-filled gorge. In times of high flow, this watercourse and its cascades—some of which

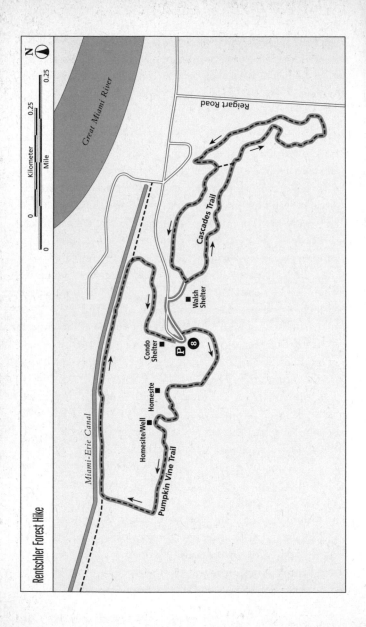

Rentschler Forest Hike

Great Miami River

Miami-Erie Canal

Reigart Road

Cascades Trail

Walsh Shelter

Condo Shelter

P 8

Homesite/Well

Homesite

Pumpkin Vine Trail

N

Kilometer
0   0.25

Mile
0   0.25

drop 8 feet—will be impressive as they spill into deep stone amphitheaters, but during summer and fall they can be dead dry. User-created trails can make this area confusing; however, just keep downstream until you reach a stone bridge over a park road. Loop back toward your parking area, passing a small plaque commemorating the addition of acreage to Rentschler Park, and a grove of planted pines.

Miles and Directions

0.0 From the parking area near the Condo Shelter, walk south toward the playground and pick up the signed Pumpkin Vine Trail and enter young woodland.

0.2 Come alongside a small clear streamlet. Watch for a homesite on the right just past the watercourse. Explore around, looking for relics, but leave them for others to enjoy.

0.3 Pass another homesite. This one has a well. Watch for wire fences.

0.4 Turn sharply north, then pass a huge white oak tree to the right of the trail.

0.5 Reach the Miami-Erie Canal. Turn right, easterly along the canal. Bridge streams off the hill to your right.

1.0 Complete the Pumpkin Vine Trail. Now head easterly toward the Walsh Shelter, then look left for the Cascades Trail leaving from its own nearby parking area.

1.2 Bridge a streambed.

1.3 Reach a trail split. Stay right, continuing southbound, bridging another larger streambed.

1.5 Curve into the stream with the cascades. Watch for falls dropping off limestone lips into circular rock amphitheaters.

1.7 Reach the stone bridge near the main park road. Turn sharply left uphill, passing a trail shortcut, then cross another tributary before entering a pine grove.

1.9 Emerge back at the Cascades Trail trailhead.

9 Gorge Trail and Lake Loop at Sharon Woods

Sharon Woods is a classic greater Cincinnati park destination. The 730-acre park has a centerpiece 35-acre lake, paddling, fishing, picnicking, and of course trails. This includes the special Gorge Trail, which travels through a natural area of Sharon Creek, with two major waterfalls where Sharon Creek cuts a chasm through the wooded landscape. A designated state natural preserve, the Sharon Creek Gorge starts your hike out right but is only 0.7 mile; therefore, pick up the paved trail that circles around Sharon Lake to complete the park experience.

Distance: 3.9-mile loop

Approximate hiking time: 2.0 to 3.0 hours

Difficulty: Moderate, mostly level

Trail surface: Gravel, natural surfaces, concrete, and asphalt

Best season: Year-round

Other trail users: Bicyclists on paved trail

Canine compatibility: Leashed dogs permitted

Fees and permits: Parking fee required

Schedule: Sunrise to sunset

Maps: Sharon Woods; USGS Glendale

Trail contacts: Hamilton County Park District, 10245 Winton Rd., Cincinnati, OH 45231; (513) 521-7275; www.greatparks.org

Finding the trailhead: From exit 46 on I-275 north of downtown Cincinnati, take US 42 south, passing Kemper Road (Sharon Woods has multiple entrances) and driving a total of 0.6 mile to Sharon Woods Road. Turn left onto Sharon Woods Road and travel 0.1 mile, then turn left onto Buckeye Falls Road. Drive for 0.3 mile and park on your left, a little ways beyond the Buckeye Shelter. The Gorge Trail starts on a nearby road turnaround (with no parking), within sight. GPS: N39° 16' 50.3", W84° 23' 59.0"

The Hike

The hike leaves the world of manicured parks and enters a mini-wilderness along Sharon Creek. The stream's clear waters flow over rocky riffles under limestone and soil banks. Rich forestland adorns the hillsides. The twenty-one–acre state nature preserve within Sharon Woods Park has not only limestone rock cliffs and waterfalls but also fossils embedded in exposed rock. Speaking of waterfalls, try to visit Sharon Creek Gorge during a deep cold spell—the frozen waterfalls are quite a sight! Conversely, the gorge will be alive with wildflowers in spring.

The first cascade is soon visible. It spills over a curved limestone lip into a rock-strewn pool. Just like any other waterfall, this one will be more spectacular at higher flows. Even though Sharon Lake is upstream of this gorge, the more water flowing into Sharon Lake the more flowing out and the more water flowing over this falls.

Continue upstream in a forest of beech, maple, and ash, enjoying more watery vistas. It is sometimes hard to believe you are surrounded by metropolitan Cincinnati while in Sharon Creek Gorge. After bridging Sharon Creek, the park golf course comes into view, compromising the wilderness effect. However, the stream continues to deliver dramatic scenery, and you pass another waterfall. This upper falls is narrower but has a deeper pool. Soon emerge from the Sharon Creek Gorge. Sharon Lake lies ahead. You now reenter a groomed park atmosphere alternating with thick woods, joining an asphalt trail curving around the impoundment.

You will be joined by many fitness walkers and also some bicyclists. In summer you'll be seeing many visitors in canoes and paddleboats on the lake.

The paved path takes you under Kemper Road and along the upper stretches of Sharon Lake before traveling under noisy I-275. The recreational footpath and utilitarian interstate display complete contrast. Bridge uppermost Sharon Creek and begin the return journey. By now one of the trailside relaxation benches may have lured you onto it. Stay in full-blown woods after leaving Sharon Lake. The hike then joins the Parcours Trail, which has exercise stations, before returning to the Buckeye Falls parking area.

Miles and Directions

0.0 From the parking area you'll see a paved path leading left. This is your return route. The Gorge Trail leaves east from the nearby road turnaround. A large informational sign is at the trail's beginning.

0.1 Reach the lower fall of Sharon Creek. An observation deck with resting bench overlooks the drop.

0.3 Bridge Sharon Creek. Note the tributary coming in near the bridge, making a waterfall of its own.

0.6 Reach an observation deck overlooking the upper falls of Sharon Creek.

0.7 Emerge from the gorge and cross Buckeye Falls Road. You are now at Sharon Lake. Turn right, joining the asphalt trail as it loops around the impoundment.

1.4 Pass an alternate parking area accessed from Kemper Road.

1.5 Spur trails lead left along the lake toward Harbor Pavilion and right up to Kemper Road.

1.6 Take a pedestrian tunnel under Kemper Road.

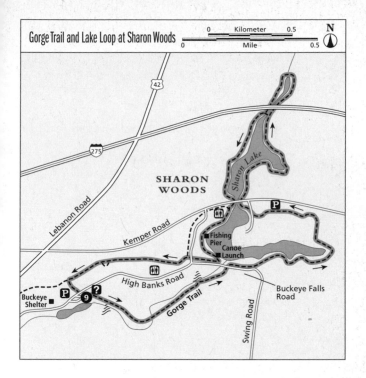

Gorge Trail and Lake Loop at Sharon Woods

SHARON WOODS

Lebanon Road

Kemper Road

High Banks Road

Gorge Trail

Buckeye Shelter

Sharon Lake

Fishing Pier

Canoe Launch

Buckeye Falls Road

Swing Road

2.1 A shortcut leads left just before the main loop passes under I-275. Continue northbound under the interstate.

2.4 Bridge upper Sharon Creek and begin returning toward the trailhead on the west bank of Sharon Lake.

2.5 Circle back under the interstate.

2.8 Pass a closed boat ramp.

3.0 Pass back under Kemper Road. Come to a junction. Stay left along Sharon Lake as another paved path leaves right. The park boat rental station is just ahead.

3.1 Pass the fishing pier.

3.2 Pass the canoe and kayak launch, then come to Buckeye Falls Road. Turn right and climb a hill, traveling westerly along Buckeye Falls Road.

3.4 Cross High Banks Road and join the wide, paved Parcours Trail.

3.7 Pass a mini-loop on the left.

3.8 Turn left onto a narrow asphalt path toward Buckeye Falls Drive. Descend.

3.9 Reach the trailhead, completing the hike.

10 Glenwood Gardens

This destination will undoubtedly surprise first-time hikers. Beyond the attractive landscaped gardens, you will enjoy an overlook before looping into the West Fork Mill Creek watershed. The hike will take you into the "back 40" of the gardens, where you will observe the flora and fauna associated with wetlands of not only West Fork Mill Creek but also several ponds and wet meadows. The lesser used trail system has enough hills to give exercise value as well as scenic beauty that will have you making return trips in different seasons.

Distance: 2.7-mile double loop
Approximate hiking time: 1.5 to 2.0 hours
Difficulty: Moderate, some hills
Trail surface: Asphalt, gravel
Best season: Spring, summer, and fall
Other trail users: None
Canine compatibility: Dogs not permitted

Fees and permits: Parking fee required
Schedule: Sunrise to sunset
Maps: Glenwood Gardens; USGS Glendale
Trail contacts: Hamilton County Park District, 10245 Winton Rd., Cincinnati, OH 45231; (513) 521-7275; www.greatparks.org

Finding the trailhead: From exit 14 on I-75 north of downtown Cincinnati, take Glendale-Milford Road west for 1.4 miles to Springfield Pike/OH 4 and a traffic light. Keep straight through the light and veer left into the gardens. (If you veer right you will enter a shopping center.) Curve around a traffic circle to reach the parking area and visitor center. GPS: N39° 15' 32.3", W84° 28' 19.8"

The Hike

Glenwood Gardens is a much-underutilized hiking destination. Perhaps it is even unrecognized as a hiking destination. Once a 360-acre working farm outside Cincinnati way back when, what was the country became city. The heirs of the farm donated land along the banks of West Fork Mill Creek to the Hamilton County parks system in 1993. Later, more acreage was added. The house and surrounding gardens were preserved and expanded. Thus, most area residents think of the gardens only when they think of this park. And it does have alluring gardens, as well as a special garden for children to learn about nature—Highfield Discovery Garden.

But there is more to Glenwood Gardens beyond the front, for Hamilton County has developed a trail system that includes a 1-mile paved loop that connects to a 1.5-mile nature trail that explores the bottomlands of West Fork Mill Creek and the woods, prairie, wetlands, and meadows along it. The parks system has systematically improved the wetland complex, resulting in a natural area with impressive summer wildflowers and an everywhere-you-look beauty that makes Glenwood Gardens an undiscovered gem of a hike amidst the heart of the urban area. That being said, take some time to amble through the gardens while you are here, before or after your hike.

You'll rarely find a more elaborate beginning to a hike, as you pass through an archway and through scenic gardens to an overlook, where the West Fork Mill Creek Valley opens before you. Attractive meadows along West Fork Mill Creek are visible, as well as part of the paved trail. The overlook reveals the lay of the land. You can see where you are going. Pass the Legacy Garden, then descend, leaving the developed gardens area to make a trail junction.

Now 99 percent of all park visitors have been left behind. Strangely, what is now scenic park terrain was once cattle country. Enjoy the level path bordered by shade trees in a mix of meadow and woodland. You will soon join the Wetland Loop, a more primitive gravel track that explores numerous ecosystems.

After bridging West Fork Mill Creek, you climb a hill then enter an area of managed wetlands. Birds and birders who watch the avian set thrive in these diverse habitats. The wet meadow area will have an amazing midsummer array of wildflowers. The lotus blooms in one pond are very color-ful. Returning to the stream, you will pass through more mixed habitats before completing the walk. Make sure to explore the developed gardens before or after your visit.

Miles and Directions

0.0 From the large parking area, walk toward the main gardens, passing through a stone archway. The Cotswold Visitor Center is to your left, but you stay right following Walking Trails signs. Shortly reach an overlook.

0.2 Pass an Indian burial mound while descending from the developed gardens. Reach a trail junction. Stay right, north-bound, on the asphalt trail. West Fork Mill Creek is to your left.

0.4 Pass a park access road. Keep straight.

0.5 Reach a trail junction. Here, the main paved loop leaves left. Turn right with the Wetland Loop, also paved. The Wetland Loop shortly bridges a stream and becomes a gravel path. Pass another park access road to the right of the trail. The main route is obvious.

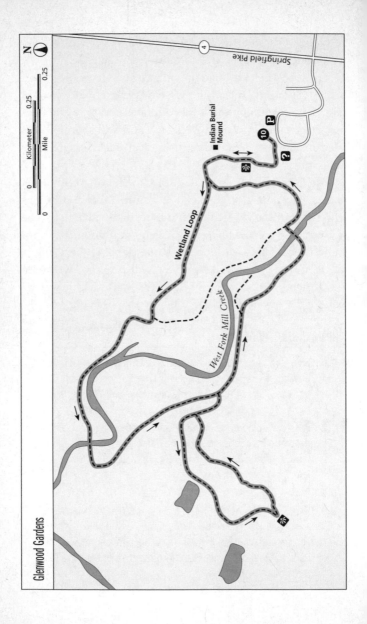

Glenwood Gardens

0.8 Cross over West Fork Mill Creek on an elaborate concrete and iron bridge in sycamore-dominated bottomland. Ascend from the stream.

0.9 Pass a four-trunked sycamore on trail right.

1.1 Take a right on a sub-loop of the Wetland Loop. Enjoy wet meadow, pond, and prairie environments.

1.2 Stay right as the trail splits on the loop proper. Ascend to pass small ponds with views from the trail.

1.5 Reach a hilltop vista and contemplation bench. Begin ambling back to West Fork Mill Creek bottoms.

1.8 Finish the mini-loop.

1.9 Stay right at an intersection, cruising down West Fork Mill Creek Valley.

2.2 Bridge West Fork Mill Creek. Enjoy open views of the stream. Next bridge a tributary on a rustic old bridge. Shortly meet the paved trail and keep right, curving below the main house and gardens.

2.5 Finish the paved loop. Turn right and backtrack uphill to the developed gardens.

2.7 Complete the hike after passing back through the developed gardens.

11 Winton Woods Hike

Big Winton Woods Park, which offers nearly every out-door recreation activity under the sun, is the setting for this hike combining two nearby nature trails. You will first hike the Kingfisher Trail. It explores wetlands along Kingfisher Creek, a tributary of West Fork Mill Creek, then climbs a hillside before dropping to the stream again, where you become one with the water, traveling its floodplain. Aquatic vistas are ample along this surprisingly scenic suburban stream. The next loop, the Great Oaks Trail, explores the same watershed but visits some huge trees from which it derives it name. Be apprised the trailheads are 0.5 mile apart but on the same road, allowing for quick foot or auto access between the two.

Distance: 1.7-mile double loop
Approximate hiking time: 1.0 to 2.0 hours
Difficulty: Moderate, some hills
Trail surface: Gravel
Best season: Year-round
Other trail users: None
Canine compatibility: Leashed dogs permitted

Fees and permits: Parking fee required
Schedule: Sunrise to sunset
Maps: Winton Woods; USGS Greenhills
Trail contacts: Hamilton County Park District, 10245 Winton Rd., Cincinnati, OH 45231; (513) 521-7275; www.greatparks.org

Finding the trailhead: From exit 39 on I-275 north of downtown Cincinnati, take Winton Road south for 2.9 miles, to turn right onto Valleyview Drive, toward the Winton Center. Follow Valleyview for 0.6 mile to the Kingfisher Shelter and picnic area. The Kingfisher Trail starts from this parking area. The Great Oaks Trail is 0.5 mile farther on Valleyview Road. GPS: N39° 15' 30.00", W84° 31' 48.66"

The Hike

Despite coming in at 2,500-plus acres, Winton Woods is somewhat lacking in rustic nature trails. It does have golfing, paddling, camping, basketball, disc golf, fishing, horseback riding, and more, including a hundred-acre demonstration farm where kids can explore orchards and gardens as well as see farm animals. So there is no recreation shortage. The park does have 3.7 miles of paved pathways, which course through the developed facilities of Winton Woods. The only two nature trails it has are included in this hike—the Kingfisher Trail and the Great Oaks Trail. So while you are here, consider hiking these two nature trails and incorporating other activities available at Winton Woods.

The Kingfisher Trail loops around a wetland along Kingfisher Creek. It first joins a hill above a meadow encircled with an encroaching forest. Locust, cherry, and tulip trees shade the path as it bisects wet weather streams draining the slope above you. Watch for sinkholes draining the hillsides. They flow underground, leaving no streambed, demonstrating the complicated underground plumbing created by Mother Nature. The young forest through which you travel was likely pasture a couple of generations past, before the park came to be.

The best part of the Kingfisher Trail comes when you begin cruising along Kingfisher Creek. The clear stream is scenic despite draining an urban area, which will inevitably leave a little trash. Note how the waterside vegetation all faces downstream—a result of flash floods. Urban streams tend to rise and fall quicker since they drain places such as streets and parking lots that don't absorb water. Wooded areas with soil, like here at Winton Woods, absorb water and hold it longer.

Curve by a bona fide wetland near the lower end of the Kingfisher Trail. These wetlands not only harbor unique vegetation but also play a role in flood control by absorbing and slowing aquatic flow.

Pick up the Great Oaks Trail after walking or driving the 0.5 mile to its trailhead. Enter big woods of oak, maple, beech, and cherry. Shortly reach its loop, and ramble among stately primeval bur oaks and beech trees. When walking along Kingfisher Creek, you are on a high slope, which offers a top-down perspective as opposed to the water-level Kingfisher Trail. Your return trip takes you uphill, away from the stream, before completing the hike.

Miles and Directions

0.0 Leave the Kingfisher Shelter parking area on a gravel track, passing through a wooden fence and up an old roadbed. Ramble north with the tributary to your left.

0.1 The trail leading left is your return route. For now, leave the old roadbed and curve right and uphill into thick woods.

0.3 Pass a limestone sinkhole on your right.

0.5 Reach the apex of the loop and begin curving back downstream. Ignore any user-created trails connecting nearby roads or to the Great Oaks Trail.

0.9 Walk a long boardwalk near Kingfisher Creek.

1.0 Complete the Kingfisher Trail loop. Backtrack toward the trailhead.

1.1 Return to the Kingfisher Shelter parking area. You can either walk the 0.5 mile to the Great Oaks Trail parking area or drive west on Valleyview Drive.

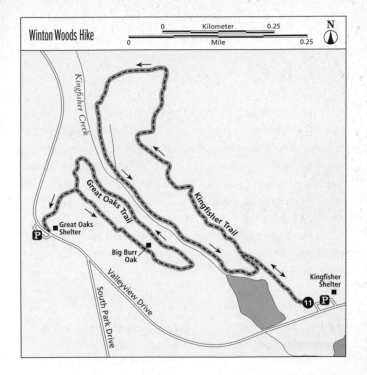

1.2 Reach the loop portion of the Great Oaks Trail. Head right, uphill, before descending toward Kingfisher Creek.

1.3 Meet a massive signed bur oak amid many other stately giants. Shortly reach the stream below and turn left, heading upstream with Kingfisher Creek to your right.

1.6 Climb away from Kingfisher Creek and keep west after making the Great Oaks Trail loop.

1.7 Arrive back at the Great Oaks Trail parking area, completing the hike.

12 Stone Steps Loop at Mount Airy Forest

This hike explores the south side of Cincinnati's historic Mount Airy Forest. Depart the historic Oval Shelter and descend a steep hollow centered by a rocky drainage. You will drop over 300 feet. Your climb back out includes using the Stone Steps, hand-placed limestone footings that help you negotiate your way directly up the nose of a ridge. The balance of the hike curves around rib ridges and into rocky drainages sloping off the side of Mount Airy. Numerous trail junctions add a navigational challenge to this rewarding hike that will leave you coming back to this trail haven for more hikes.

Distance: 2.8-mile loop

Approximate hiking time: 1.5 to 2.5 hours

Difficulty: Moderate, but with steep hills

Trail surface: Natural surfaces

Best season: Year-round

Other trail users: None

Canine compatibility: Leashed dogs permitted

Fees and permits: No fees or permits required

Schedule: Sunrise to sunset

Maps: Mount Airy Forest; USGS Cincinnati West

Trail contacts: Cincinnati Parks, 950 Eden Park Dr., Cincinnati, OH 45202; (513) 352-4080; www.cincyparks.com

Finding the trailhead: From exit 18 on I-74 northwest of downtown Cincinnati, emerge from the interstate to reach the intersection of West Fork and Colerain Avenue, US 27. Take Colerain Avenue, US 27, north for 1.4 miles to enter Mount Airy Forest. Turn left into the forest then immediately turn left onto Trail Ridge Road and reach the Oval at 0.4 mile. Circle three-quarters the way around the oval to reach the Red Oak Trail, on the outside of the road. Pick up the Red Oak Trail as it descends into woodland. GPS: N39° 10' 22.0", W84° 34' 4.2"

The Hike

This hike takes place at the city of Cincinnati's largest park, Mount Airy Forest, now officially listed on the National Register of Historic Places. A century ago, the park was small farms on a big hill of Colerain Avenue. Poor agricultural practices turned the hill into naked ground eroding at an alarming rate. The city began purchasing the farms and replanted over 1,200,000 trees! They also stabilized eroded land. And by 1914, the *Cincinnati Times Star* boasted, "It is no exaggeration to say that Mount Airy Forest comprises the most picturesque assortment of hills, valleys, streams, woods, lawns, and wild scenery that we have within the city limits." During the 1930s the Civilian Conservation Corps built most of the rustic park structures we see today, which added to the literally growing natural beauty as the trees blossomed into the gorgeous forest we see today. Nearly all Cincinnatians—even nonpark visitors—have seen the stone walls along Colerain Avenue built by the CCC.

The CCC also built the stone steps that are one of the highlights of this hike. The veinlike trail network on the 1,459-acre park (40 percent of the total city park acreage) is big enough that you definitely need a map; otherwise, you may find yourself hiking in circles. Trail junctions are well marked, but you will need the map to confirm your position. Download a complete park trail map from the above listed Cincinnati Parks website before starting your trek.

The single-track Red Oak Trail takes you from the Oval down to the bottom of the hill. The hollow to your right increases in size as you drop. Sounds of the city drift into the woods, but your visual perceptions will be nothing but natural. Enjoy the Stone Steps, even though it is uphill. From there, you will navigate a plethora of junctions, but you are never far from the Oval (where you parked) in case you get discombobulated. Even at that, you will see the allure of the locale and return to Mount Airy Forest to create your own loop.

Miles and Directions

0.0 Leave the Oval, southbound on the Red Oak Trail.

0.2 Keep straight at your first trail intersection. Keep downhill and step over a streambed. And keep straight at the next junction just ahead.

0.8 Descend to cross a bridge over the hollow you have been paralleling, then open onto a field not far from West Fork Road. Look right for the Ponderosa Trail and begin regaining the elevation you lost.

0.9 Reach the Stone Steps. Make the lung-busting climb straight up the nose of a ridge on limestone steps.

1.0 Stay left at a three-way junction shortly after the Stone Steps, now on a level track.

1.4 Make a four-way junction shortly. Keep straight.

1.8 Turn right at a three-way junction. Shortly meet Trail Ridge Road. Cross the road and veer right, passing through a picnic area with a water spigot. Join a spur leading downhill to the Furnas Trail. Just downhill, meet the Furnas Trail and turn right, northbound.

2.1 Pass a narrow trail coming up from West Fork Road.

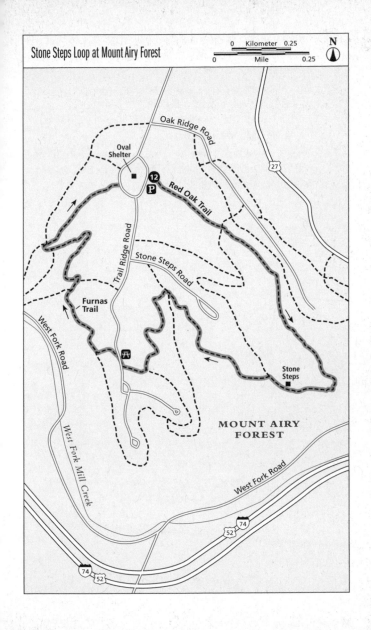

Stone Steps Loop at Mount Airy Forest

N

0   Kilometer   0.25
0   Mile   0.25

Oak Ridge Road

27

Oval
Shelter

12
P

Red Oak Trail

Trail Ridge Road

Stone Steps Road

Furnas
Trail

West Fork Road

West Fork Mill Creek

Stone
Steps

MOUNT AIRY
FOREST

West Fork Road

74
52

74
52

2.2 Pass a trail leaving right, uphill, to Trail Ridge Road. Ahead, curve around a hollow. Watch for hemlock trees, rare in these parts.

2.5 Pass a trail leading left and downhill. Stay right with the Furnas Trail. Circle around a big sinkhole and pass two more junctions; stay right, avoiding the trail to the Treehouse and taking the trail toward the Oval.

2.8 Emerge on the west side of the Oval, away from your starting point. Head toward the shelter in the middle of the Oval and walk a few feet to the trail's beginning.

13 Caldwell Preserve Hike

Caldwell Preserve is a protected natural portion of Caldwell Park. The preserve is centered on three tributaries of Mill Creek and steep ridges that divide them. Primitive single-track footpaths ramble throughout the densely wooded landscape. The hike explores the highs and low of the preserve, first crossing Ravine Creek then exploring two ridges that offer partial views into the lands below. Finally, it dips to the floodplain along Mill Creek, where cottonwoods rise from the creek bottom. A final ascent returns you to the trailhead.

Distance: 2.2-mile loop
Approximate hiking time: 1.5 to 2.0 hours
Difficulty: Moderate, has hills
Trail surface: Mostly natural surfaces
Best season: Year-round
Other trail users: None
Canine compatibility: No dogs allowed

Fees and permits: No fees or permits required
Schedule: Sunrise to sunset
Maps: Caldwell Park; USGS Cincinnati East
Trail contacts: Cincinnati Parks, 950 Eden Park Dr., Cincinnati, OH 45202; (513) 352-4080; www.cincyparks.com

Finding the trailhead: From exit 9 on I-75 north of downtown Cincinnati, take Paddock Road northwest from the interstate for 0.1 mile to North Bend Road. Turn left onto North Bend Road and follow it for 1.0 mile to the nature center, on your right. **Note:** Do not turn right into Caldwell Park Playground. Continue on North Bend Road after bridging Mill Creek then reach the preserve. GPS: N39° 12' 5.43", W84° 29' 32.72"

The Hike

The land where Caldwell Preserve lies has a long history. Nearly 350 acres were initially purchased by James Caldwell in the late 1700s. The Caldwell family held on to it into the early 1900s, when 122 acres went to the city of Cincinnati to be used as a park. This was about the time Mount Airy Forest got started and Cincinnati was getting serious about obtaining parkland in the fast-growing metropolis before outward development made land purchases for parks so expensive the city couldn't afford it. The Caldwell heirs generously donated the land. The park has been used for many things and today contains three distinct units—a golf course, playground, and the nature preserve, where this hike takes place.

The preserve has a nature center, where area residents, primarily schoolchildren, learn about the environment. And there is plenty to see here, including old-growth forest, wildflowers along streams, both year-round and migratory birds, even deer. The varied habitats, from the bottoms of Mill Creek to its flowing tributaries to the steep ridges to open meadows, help sustain the biodiversity. And you can see them all as a network of trails explores the entirety of habitats.

This hike first visits the cool spring-fed Ravine Creek, a rocky rill feeding Mill Creek. It then climbs to a ridge where you explore old-growth woodlands on the aptly named Paw Paw Ridge Loop Trail. Big trees tower over the leaf-laden pawpaws. Enjoy a view into the watershed below before completing the loop and curving out to another ridge where another view extends east across the Mill Creek Valley.

The hike then drops back to Ravine Creek, where you pass a rocked-in spring before coming along Mill Creek. A spur trail leads to the water's edge of this large stream that drains much of Cincinnati. A final uphill push leads you back to the trailhead.

Miles and Directions

0.0 Leave from the parking auto turnaround near the nature center on the Ray Abercrombie Trail. Take a gravel all-accessible track in maple-oak woods. Watch for a huge oak here.

0.1 Turn right, going down wood steps to cross Ravine Creek. Turn left onto the Ravine Trail.

0.2 Leave right from the Ravine Trail, ascending earth-and-wood steps to a ridge. Level off at a trail junction and old concrete service drive. Keep straight here, beginning the Paw Paw Loop Trail. Ignore spur to the golf course. Pass some huge beech trees.

0.5 The Paw Paw Loop Trail splits. Stay right, heading toward Mill Creek. Big trees tower overhead.

0.8 Reach the end of the bluff over Mill Creek. Curve west to pass a developed overlook rising above the chasm below.

1.0 Complete the loop portion of Paw Paw Trail. Backtrack to the old service drive, then curve left, easterly, on the Ray Abercrombie Loop Trail. Stay left as it soon splits.

1.6 Reach a spur trail leading left to an overlook of Mill Creek after passing a shortcut trail leading toward Ravine Creek. Enjoy good winter views of Mill Creek floodplain below from a nearly sheer drop-off.

1.7 Stay left, passing two junctions to reach the Ravine Creek Trail. Bridge Ravine Creek, then head downstream.

1.8 Pass a rocked-in spring that trickles across the trail. Continue downstream, bridging a tributary and intersecting a trail leading right up "Killer Hill," so named after an out-of-shape teacher said she was going to die while climbing it. The hike then opens onto the Mill Creek bottoms. User-created trails

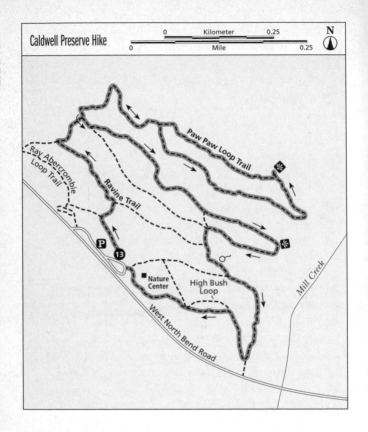

Caldwell Preserve Hike

lead to the creek. Look for huge cottonwood trees in the bottoms.

2.0 Turn right and climb a hill, as a spur trail leads forward a few feet to North Bend Road. Meet the High Bush Loop as it splits. Stay left. Follow the High Bush Loop back toward the nature center.

2.2 Emerge near the back of the nature center, completing the hike.

14 French Park

Many Cincinnati hikers believe the stream flowing through French Park to be the most scenic in the city. They cite its numerous cascades, its frozen winter beauty, and the wildflowers that spring forth from its banks. The trail along French Creek may be described as a "water walk," as you must step over the watercourse several times. The water walk is only part of the trek. First, you will walk along another tributary, then circle the park's highland perimeter, saving your water walk for last.

Distance: 3.3-mile lollipop

Approximate hiking time: 2.0 to 3.0 hours

Difficulty: Moderate, has hills

Trail surface: Natural surfaces

Best season: Year-round

Other trail users: None

Canine compatibility: Leashed dogs permitted

Fees and permits: No fees or permits required

Schedule: Sunrise to sunset

Maps: French Park; USGS Cincinnati East

Trail contacts: Cincinnati Parks, 950 Eden Park Dr., Cincinnati, OH 45202; (513) 352-4080; www.cincyparks.com

Finding the trailhead: From exit 12 on I-71 northeast of downtown Cincinnati, take Montgomery Road/US 22/OH 3 south for 1.6 miles to Ohio Avenue and a traffic light. Turn right onto Ohio Avenue and travel just a short distance to Section Road. Turn left onto Section Road and follow it west for 1.1 miles. Turn right into the park, passing a parking area. Continue up the main park road, circling behind the French House. At 0.2 mile, just beyond the manor, turn right onto the one-way exit road, following it downhill to a parking area on your left, just before returning to Section Road. GPS: N39° 11' 44.87", W84° 25' 28.93"

The Hike

French Park was originally an estate centered with a large red-brick manor you see today. Originally built in the early 1900s and remodeled numerous times since then, the dwelling is now available for event rental from the city of Cincinnati. The house and grounds were donated to the city in 1943. The mostly forested park is groomed around the house but also includes a section of restored prairie. A picnic shelter at the top of a hill, which you will come near on your hike, offers a far-reaching view to the west and is worth checking out.

Most of the time you will be circling the perimeter of the 275-acre preserve, though the water walk travels through the heart of French Park. The trails themselves are in pretty fair shape, though the numerous trail junctions combined with a few user-created paths can make things slightly confusing for first-time hikers. However, the close proximity of the park border, which is surrounded by houses and also the park roads and other nearby roads, make being lost for very long an unlikely proposition.

You first join the Sierra Trail, named for the Sierra Club, which constructed it in 1992. A prairie to your left offers large and colorful wildflowers in summer. Soon enter woodland, traveling easterly along a streamlet, which is a tributary of French Creek, which is a tributary of Mill Creek, which is a tributary of the Ohio River. Soon climb the park's big hill. Note the planted evergreens in the woods. Ahead, pass side trails leading to the shelter atop the hill. Go visit the shelter and take in the westerly view, where you can perhaps see to Indiana on a clear fall or winter day.

You then get your first taste of French Creek, spanning it on a bridge before you resume your circumnavigation of the park grounds. Enjoy traipsing through a meadow, which offers blackberries in summertime. Next you'll join the Creek Trail, which parallels French Creek, with its small cascades dropping over layer after layer of rock strata. You will have numerous crossings, but most of them can be rock hopped with dry feet except after heavy rains and occasional wet periods in winter and spring. If the crossings seem too difficult, simply follow the main park road behind the French House and walk to your vehicle.

Miles and Directions

0.0 From the parking area near Section Road at the end of the one-way road after passing the French House, take the Sierra Trail, heading east.

0.3 Turn left, curving uphill along the park border, gaining 100 feet in elevation in a short distance.

0.5 Pass the first of three spur trails leading left to the park shelter. A big view opens near the shelter. Keep north along the park boundary.

0.8 Descend to reach French Creek. A bridge spans this upper part of the creek. Begin the loop portion of the hike. Take a few steps downstream then curve right, away from the creek heading uphill on wood-and-earth steps. Just ahead, pass a trail leading left—stay right.

1.0 The main outside loop turns west.

1.2 Reach a trail junction in an open brushy area. The trail leading left heads to the lower parking area. Keep straight, but now on a grassy track.

1.4 Meet a cell tower service road. Turn right, tracing the service road.

1.6 Leave left from the service road, back on trail. Soon enter an open meadow in the process of becoming reforested.

1.9 Reach the lower parking area. Turn left onto the park road,

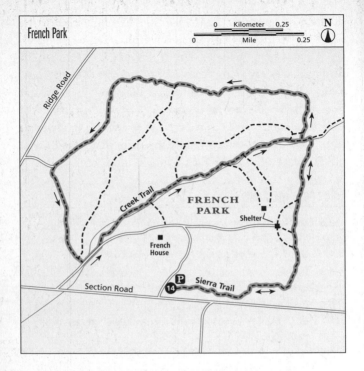

French Park

bridging French Creek. Leave the road left, passing through a shady picnic area to pick up the Creek Trail. Immediately rock hop French Creek. Enjoy the clear stream as it flows over a limestone bed in numerous shoals divided by pools.

2.1 A spur trail leaves right and uphill to the French House.

2.2 A spur trail leads left; keep straight.

2.3 A spur trail leads right uphill toward the picnic shelter. Ahead, a second spur leads toward the picnic shelter.

2.5 Complete the loop portion of the hike. Cross the bridge over French Creek then backtrack on the Sierra Trail to the trailhead.

3.3 Reach the trailhead, completing the hike.

15 Red Fox Trail

This easy hike explores bottomlands adjacent to Stonelick Lake, at Stonelick State Park. The loop leaves from the park campground traveling through sometimes–wet flatwoods before opening to the upper reaches of Stonelick Lake. An old roadbed creates an artificial peninsula extending into the water. Your return route traces old roads part of the way. Spur paths lead to the park campground and amphitheater.

Distance: 1.8-mile loop
Approximate hiking time: 1.0 to 1.5 hours
Difficulty: Easy
Trail surface: Natural surfaces
Best season: Late summer, fall
Other trail users: Bicyclists
Canine compatibility: Leashed dogs permitted

Fees and permits: No fees or permits required
Schedule: Sunrise to sunset
Maps: Stonelick State Park; USGS Newtonsville
Trail contacts: Stonelick State Park, 2895 Lake Dr., Pleasant Plain, OH 45162; (513) 734-4323; www.dnr.state.oh.us/

Finding the trailhead: From exit 59A on I-275, take Milford Parkway north 1.0 mile to meet US 50 and OH 131 at a light. Keep straight through the light to join OH 131 east for 8.5 miles to OH 727. Veer left onto OH 727 and follow it for 3.1 miles to Lake Drive. Turn right onto Lake Drive and follow it toward Camping, Beach, Picnic Area, Boat Rental. Enter the park after 0.3 mile. Keep straight, following Lake Drive 2.0 miles toward the campground. The Red Fox Trail starts on your right, within sight of the campground check-in station. To park, pass the check-in station and turn left into a parking area. GPS: N39° 12' 59.58", W84° 3' 22.81"

The Hike

This hike is enjoyable as a stand-alone event, but if you are going to visit Stonelick State Park, why not add to the adventure by enjoying other aspects of the waterside getaway northeast of Cincinnati?

The park is known for its fossils embedded in some ancient rock that rises to the surface. The rock is known as the Cincinnati Arch. Not an arch in the conventional sense, it is actually a dome of rock that has risen to the earth's surface and was exposed through erosion. This rock has attracted students of fossils since the 1800s. Later, the area was seen as a potential recreation destination. In 1948 the state began acquiring land around Stonelick Creek, which was dammed in 1950, creating Stonelick Lake, the park's centerpiece. Today the park offers not only hiking but also water sports such as boating and fishing. They also have a designated swim beach.

The Red Fox Trail enters woods, leaving the campground area. Beech, cedar, and sweet gum trees provide cover. Both red maple and sugar maple can be found here. Distinguishing between sugar maples and red maples is easy. Look at the leaf of a sugar maple. The curves between lobes of the sugar maple are U-shaped, whereas the curves between lobes of the red maple are at right angles.

Club moss, a green ground cover, creeps across the forest floor. The flat track provides great contrast to the hilly hiking trails near the Ohio River. Unfortunately, water can collect and make the track muddy in spots. Avoid this hike after rainy periods unless you like sloshing in your boots.

The rooty path begins aiming for Stonelick Lake after passing a shortcut. Come along the water and gain lakeside views. Meet an old roadbed that forms a peninsula jutting into Stonelick Lake. Take this spur for a good aquatic vista, then resume your loop, leaving the impoundment. Return through flatwoods to the Red Fox Trail's beginning.

The park has a few other hiking trails, too, in case you want to further stretch your legs. They all link, as well. The Beechtree Trail starts near the park entrance and winds 1.5 miles to meet the Southwoods Trail and the Lakeview Trail. The Lakeview Trail, as its name implies, runs along the shore of Stonelick Lake for 1.0 mile. The Southwoods Trail, 0.8 mile long, connects this hike—the Red Fox Trail—to the Lakeview and Beechtree Trails.

Miles and Directions

0.0 From the north side of the road just east of the campground entrance station, take the signed Red Fox Trail heading north into flatwoods.

0.1 The Red Fox Trail forks. Stay right, still on a level path.

0.3 Cross a streambed on a small iron bridge to reach a trail junction. Here, a shortcut leaves arrow-straight left—it is an old roadbed—while the main loop keeps straight. Soon come fairly near OH 13 before turning northwest.

0.8 Reach a trail junction. The more heavily used path leads left, while a fainter trail leads right. Stay right on the fainter trail and shortly come to Stonelick Lake. Cruise along the shoreline.

1.0 Reach an old roadbed. Turn right to reach a lake view on a peninsula, then follow it away from the lake on a slight incline.

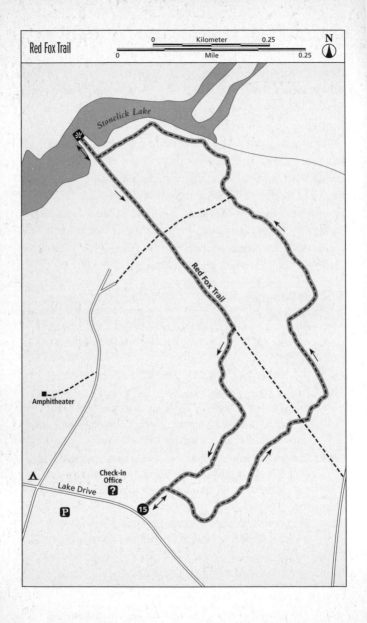

Red Fox Trail

Stonelick Lake

Red Fox Trail

Amphitheater

Lake Drive

Check-in Office
?

15

0   Kilometer   0.25
0   Mile   0.25

N

1.2 Reach a four-way junction. Keep straight on the old road-bed. The grassy track leading right heads to the park campground and amphitheater.

1.4 Reach a three-way trail junction. Turn right, back toward the park campground.

1.7 Complete the loop portion of the hike. Keep straight.

1.8 Emerge on the paved park road, completing the trail.

16 Fern Hill Trail

This woodsy ramble meanders through hills above East Fork Lake at East Fork Lake State Park. The narrow footpath crosses a rocky stream cutting a deep hollow, which you ascend. Pass a big white oak tree and skirt around the head of the hollow before passing near the park campground. The final part travels through former farm country before returning to the trailhead.

Distance: 1.4-mile loop
Approximate hiking time: 1.0 to 1.5 hours
Difficulty: Easy
Trail surface: Natural surfaces
Best season: Year-round
Other trail users: None
Canine compatibility: Leashed dogs permitted

Fees and permits: Entrance fee required
Schedule: Sunrise to sunset
Maps: East Fork State Park Trail Guide; USGS Williamsburg
Trail contacts: East Fork State Park, 3294 Elklick Rd., Bethel, OH 45106; (513) 734-4323; www.dnr.state.oh.us/

Finding the trailhead: From exit 63B on I-275 east of downtown Cincinnati, take OH 32 east, Appalachian Highway, for 10.5 miles to exit at Half Acre Road. Follow Half Acre Road south for 0.8 mile to reach Old State Road 32. Turn left onto Old State Road 32 and follow it for 0.1 mile to turn right into the state park on Park Road 4. Follow Park Road 4 for 0.4 mile to Park Road 5. Turn left on Park Road 5, following signs to the campground. At 0.4 mile, pass by the campground entrance station, paying your entrance fee, then keep forward through the campground for a total of 2.3 miles on Park Road 5 to reach a gated road on the left toward the closed campground swim beach. Park here (you can park in front of the gate). The signed Fern Hill Trail starts downhill from the gated left turn to the closed campground swim beach. You will come to a boat ramp and the end of the road if you have gone too far. The boat ramp offers additional parking. GPS: N39° 1' 29.03", W84° 5' 40.25"

The Hike

East Fork State Park has an impressive array of trails, including hiking, equestrian, mountain biking, and even backpacking trails. Many are multiuse trails. Fern Hill Trail, a hiking-only path near the park campground, sometimes gets lost in the mix. But once you have found it, the loop will be on your list of "to do" hikes here at the state park. There are some trails you will want to avoid here on the park's north half, primarily the equestrian trails, which are heavily used and can be quite muddy.

This hike investigates forested hills and moist hollows where rocky streams can be found, and lies between East Fork Little Miami River to the east and Cabin Run to the west. The state park offers a varied landscape that, combined with the large trail network, adds up to a lot of hiking variety. The park also has wide flat floodplains grown up in woodlands, high bluffs above East Fork, prairie and grassland, and lots of land transitioning to forest from farm use.

The path starts narrow and stays narrow throughout its entirety. Initially run parallel to the lake shoreline a few hundred feet back. Bridge small branches trickling toward the lake. A thicket of cedar, walnut, maple, cherry, and vines suffocates the path during the growing season. You will see plenty of ferns on the forest floor. Even during the thickness of summer, you can still gain glimpses of the lake.

The path wanders up a moist hollow that makes for a good spring wildflower area. Come near the state park campground. Look around for barbwire and other relics of when this was farmland. The woods here are clearly younger and stay that way to the hike's end.

East Fork is one of Ohio's largest state parks, coming in at nearly 5,000 acres. East Fork Lake, also known as Harsha Lake, is the centerpiece of the park. The impoundment was created to prevent disastrous floods on East Fork Little Miami River. The lake itself is over 2,000 acres in size and is popular with motorboaters during the warm season and anglers seemingly year-round as they vie for smallmouth bass, bluegill, and crappie, as well as largemouth bass and stripers. Other watery pursuits include swimming. The park offers a large swimming beach that is popular with kids and adults alike. Since you are already at the lake, combine your hike with watery pursuits or a camping adventure.

Miles and Directions

0.0 From the north side of the road just past the gated road to the old campground swim beach, take the signed Fern Hill Trail heading north into dense forest.

0.3 Step over the major unnamed tributary flowing across the path. Climb away from the unnamed tributary and pass a huge white oak just to the right of the trail.

0.6 Pick up some hand-laid limestone steps and climb deeper in the hollow.

0.7 Circle around the head of the hollow and cross the tributary one more time. The forest is younger here and was likely pastureland before the lake and park were established.

0.9 Come very near Campsite #397, which is part of the K Loop. Watch for bootleg trails crisscrossing the main path, created when campers hunt for wood. Ahead, come out beside the K Loop, then continue circling around it before resuming a southbound direction.

1.2 Briefly pick up an arrow-straight roadbed. Descend.

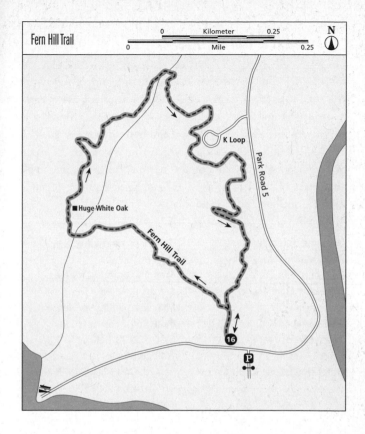

1.3 Complete the loop portion of the hike. Keep left.

1.4 Emerge on the park road, completing the trail.

17 East Fork Loop

This 5-mile circuit explores rolling terrain, much of it along the south shore of East Fork Lake at East Fork State Park. Using a combination of the park's Backpack Trail and the Newman Trail, hikers will be impressed with the variety of flora and landscapes through which they stroll. Be apprised you will be sharing part of the trail at the beginning with mountain bikers and at the very end with equestrians. The balance of the trek is hiker only.

Distance: 5.0-mile loop

Approximate hiking time: 2.5 to 3.5 hours

Difficulty: More challenging due to distance

Trail surface: Natural surfaces

Best season: Year-round, good fall color trail

Other trail users: Mountain bikers, equestrians

Canine compatibility: Leashed dogs permitted

Fees and permits: No fees or permits required

Schedule: Sunrise to sunset

Maps: East Fork State Park Trail Guide; USGS Batavia

Trail contacts: East Fork State Park, 3294 Elklick Rd., Bethel, OH 45106; (513) 734-4323; www.dnr.state.oh.us/

Finding the trailhead: From exit 65 on I-275 east of downtown Cincinnati, take OH 125 east for 10.0 miles to Bantam Road and a traffic light. Turn left onto Bantam Road and follow it 0.2 mile, then turn left into the state park on Park Road 1. Follow Park Road 1 for 0.5 mile, passing the park office on your right, to the left turn for Mountain Bike Trail, Backpack Trail Access. This is known as the south trailhead. Turn left and follow the gravel road just a short distance to a dead end. GPS: N39° 0' 24.1", W84° 8' 31.0"

The Hike

This is the longest hike in this entire guide and is the most challenging too. It takes place at big East Fork State Park, which offers a plethora of trails whether you are a mountain biker, equestrian, backpacker, or day hiker. It also has camping, boating, fishing, and swimming. This hike combines portions of two of its longest trails, the 8-mile Backpack Trail and the 32-mile Steven Newman World Walker Perimeter Trail, commonly known as the Newman Trail or the Perimeter Trail.

During its 5-mile trek this hike travels through a multiplicity of environments with a great assortment of trees, which makes it a great fall hike destination. It begins in flatwoods, then dips to a stream. This rocky watercourse with steep bluffs can run from a torrent to a trickle depending upon the season. Curve in and out of hollows that feed it, shaded by sugar maples galore. Later you will enjoy some lakeside terrain. Parts of the hike travel a high bluff overlooking the old riverbed of East Fork Little Miami River, the watercourse impounded by East Fork Lake. The trail also ambles through former farmland that is now becoming reforested since it is now out of use. However, the vast majority of the hike is under a tree canopy.

The trails are well marked, and you will also benefit from bridges spanning many streambeds. Along the way you will come to a designated backcountry campsite. This loop would be a great beginner's backpack for those who want to expand beyond day hiking and get a feel for camping out while on the trail. The campsite has a pit toilet, fire ring, trail shelter, and tent sites. Bring your own water, which you could cache at one of the road crossings.

Miles and Directions

0.0   From the south trailhead join the red-blazed Backpack Trail, heading north into spindly straight flatwoods. This part of the hike is shared with the Mountain Bike Trail.

0.2   The trail forks. The main portion of the yellow-blazed Mountain Bike Trail leaves left. Stay right with the Backpack Trail as it dips into a hollow.

0.5   Step over the rocky stream cutting through the hollow. Begin roughly tracing the stream you just crossed toward East Fork Lake. Wander in and out of small hollows.

1.3   Come near East Fork Lake with views. It is but a short downhill walk to reach the water.

2.0   The Technical Trail, another mountain bike path, keeps straight while the Backpack Trail curves left to bridge a small drainage. For the next couple of miles the loop is hiker only.

2.4   Cross Park Road 3. Winter views of the lake open up to the main body of East Fork Lake. Pass among many hickories. Come alongside the edge of a steep drainage.

2.9   Pass an old homesite to the left of the trail before crossing Park Road 2. Come alongside a picnic area.

3.1   Saddle up to a high bluff above the lake. Trace the curve of the bluff. Spur trails lead right, uphill, to the picnic area.

3.2   A spur trail drops left, very sharply downhill to a picnic table and on to the lake. Stay with the red-blazed Backpack Trail.

3.8   Reach a trail junction. Here, the Backpack Trail leaves left. You turn right with the Overnight Connector Trail. Immediately cross Park Road 1. Begin cruising westerly in flatwoods on an old roadbed.

4.2   Reach the backcountry campsite, Camp 1. After leaving the campsite, join a spur of the Newman Trail, which is open to equestrians and hikers.

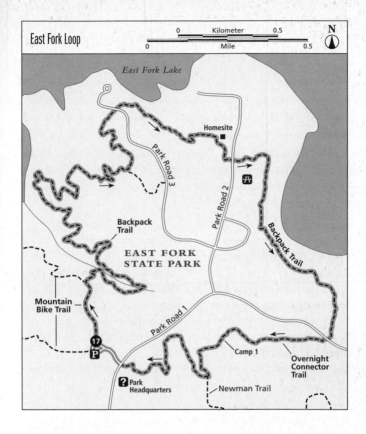

East Fork Loop

0 Kilometer 0.5
0 Mile 0.5

N

East Fork Lake

Homesite

Park Road 3

Park Road 2

Backpack Trail

EAST FORK STATE PARK

Backpack Trail

Mountain Bike Trail

17
P

Park Road 1

Camp 1

Overnight Connector Trail

? Park Headquarters

Newman Trail

4.3 Cross a stony streambed then join the Newman Trail. Turn right, westbound. Enter old farmland in various stages of succession.

4.8 Curve behind the park headquarters.

4.9 Cross Park Road 1. Follow the gravel road toward the south trailhead.

5.0 Reach the south trailhead, completing the loop.

18 Sycamore Park Lollipop

This is a scenic and underused hike at a well-groomed Clermont County park. Cruise along the banks of East Fork Little Miami River, passing rock rapids between quiet pools in a wildflower-rich vale. Enter the James L. and Francis Wilson Nature Preserve, where the trails are a little more primitive. Eventually, turn away from the stream, climbing to a high wooded ridge before returning riverside to enjoy more of the East Fork.

Distance: 2.3-mile lollipop
Approximate hiking time: 1.5 to 2.0 hours
Difficulty: Moderate, has hills
Trail surface: Gravel and natural surfaces
Best season: Year-round
Other trail users: None
Canine compatibility: Leashed dogs permitted

Fees and permits: No fees or permits required
Schedule: Sunrise to sunset
Maps: Sycamore Park; USGS Batavia
Trail contacts: Clermont County Parks, 4082 State Route 132, Batavia, OH 45103; (513) 876-9013; www.parks.clermont countyohio.gov

Finding the trailhead: From exit 63B on I-275 east of downtown Cincinnati, take OH 32 east, Appalachian Highway, for 6.0 miles to exit for OH 132/OH 222. Take OH 132/OH 222 south for 1.5 miles (passing through Batavia) to reach the left turn into Sycamore Park. The trail system starts on the right-hand side of the park as you enter. GPS: N39° 4' 2.41", W84° 11' 16.94"

The Hike

It seems there are many Miami Rivers in the greater Cincinnati area. You have the Great Miami River, the Little

Miami River, and the East Fork Little Miami River. This hike takes place along the banks of the latter, in Clermont County, near the town of Batavia. Sycamore Park features over a mile of water frontage along the East Fork Little Miami River, which by the way flows into the Little Miami River, which flows into the Ohio River east of downtown Cincinnati. The Great Miami River flows into the Ohio River west of downtown.

The trail system is marked with plastic posts with color-coded dots indicating the different trails. Leave the developed traditional part of the park, with facilities such as a playground, picnic shelter, picnic area, and asphalt walking track, crossing a $57,000 iron bridge over a tributary of the East Fork Little Miami River. Just downstream you can see an old low-water concrete bridge spanning the same tributary. Enter the trail-laden segment of Sycamore Park. The area was a later park acquisition. With the nearby hills, extensive water frontage, and a twenty-five-acre island in the middle of the river, the state of Ohio thought it an important purchase to help preserve water quality, as well as provide green space and a venue for outdoor recreation. The state gave Clermont County a grant to purchase this land, which definitely fits all the parameters listed above.

The Wildflower Loop takes you along the river, which is singing over stony shoals. Note that the area has summer wildflowers as well as spring wildflowers. Cross a couple of wet weather tributaries, then pass a forgotten stone structure and decide what you think it used to be. Ahead, the hike enters the James L. and Francis Wilson Nature Preserve. Cruise a flat nestled between the East Fork Miami River to your left and wooded hills to your right. Make your way to the waterway via one of several access spurs before the route leaves the East Fork and travels above Lucy Run, a tributary.

The climb begins, and you make your way to the ridgecrest then loop back to East Fork. Hickory, maple, and oak predominate in the uplands. Skirt some farmland, which offers a visual alternative to the natural parklands. Not to say that farms are bad—we all need to eat.

Miles and Directions

0.0 From the south side of Sycamore Park, look for an iron bridge leaving the main parking area. Cross the bridge, passing a trailside kiosk, then begin walking upstream along the East Fork Little Miami River.

0.1 The loop portion of the Wildflower Loop leaves right, uphill. Keep straight. In spring, take the Wildflower Loop.

0.2 Pass the other end of the Wildflower Loop. Just ahead, the gravel track ends and you enter the James L. and Frances Wilson Nature Preserve. The trailbed changes from gravel to natural surface.

0.4 Reach the loop portion of your hike, the Outer Loop Trail. Your return route is coming in from the hills. For now keep forward, enjoying more of the riverside scenery. Step over a very rocky tributary.

0.5 The Ridgetop Trail comes in on your right. Keep straight, still on the river on the Outer Loop. Pass a small picnic area near the site of an old swinging bridge that crossed the river onto the twenty-five-acre island that is also part of the park. Ahead, a couple of spur trails dead-end at the water's edge.

0.7 The trail splits as you climb; stay left, closest to the East Fork. Watch for the concrete block foundation of an old house.

0.8 The trails come back together; continue climbing above the river.

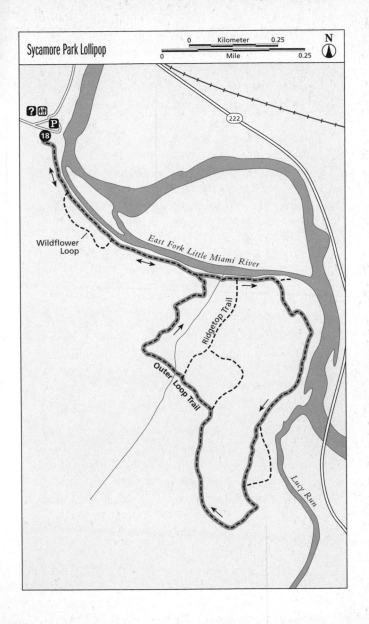

Sycamore Park Lollipop

0 Kilometer 0.25
0 Mile 0.25

N

222

18

Wildflower Loop

East Fork Little Miami River

Ridgetop Trail

Outer Loop Trail

Lucy Run

0.9 A road drops left to a meadow beside Lucy Run, but the narrower main trail keeps on the hillside. A trail soon comes back from Lucy Run.

1.1 Begin the real hill climb.

1.4 The Ridgetop Trail leaves right. Stay left, still on the Outer Loop.

1.5 The trail splits again. Stay left, descending to rock hop a stony streambed. Curve downhill toward the East Fork.

1.8 Complete the Outer Loop. Turn left and backtrack toward the developed part of Sycamore Park.

2.3 Complete the hike after crossing the iron bridge back to the parking area.

19 Withrow Preserve Walk

Travel an interconnected series of paths through a mix of environments, from hilly flower-filled woods to steep hollows shaded by big trees to level green fields left over from agricultural days to 200-foot bluffs. Different times of year will bring different rewards on this nicely maintained Hamilton County park.

Distance: 2.3-mile double loop
Approximate hiking time: 1.5 to 2.0 hours
Difficulty: Easy
Trail surface: Gravel
Best season: Year-round, spring for wildflowers
Other trail users: None
Canine compatibility: Leashed dogs permitted

Fees and permits: Parking fee required
Schedule: Sunrise to sunset
Maps: Withrow Nature Preserve; USGS Newport, Withamsville
Trail contacts: Hamilton County Park District, 10245 Winton Rd., Cincinnati, OH 45231; (513) 521-7275; www.greatparks.org

Finding the trailhead: From exit 71 on I-275 east of downtown Cincinnati, take US 52 east for 0.2 mile to turn right onto Kellogg Avenue. Follow Kellogg Avenue for 0.1 mile to turn right onto Five Mile Road. Follow Five Mile Road for 1.7 miles to the preserve. Turn right and follow the park road to a large parking area near Highwood Lodge. GPS: N39° 3' 5.99", W84° 22' 35.13"

The Hike

Many highlights are included in this hike, namely a cleared view of the Ohio River, meadows where you may see wildlife, a little farm history, big trees, and wildflowers in season. And you might get to see a wedding, as the High-wood Lodge, the on-site private house turned public event building, often holds the ceremonies.

But they don't call it Withrow Nature Preserve for nothing. The 270-acre property sits on a crest between Five Mile Creek to the north and the Ohio River to the south. The overwhelming majority of the property is in a natural state, exceptions being a small tract around the house that is kept groomed and also some fields left over from farming days. One negative: I-275 is a little too close, and road noise from the interstate drifts into the preserve.

The hike first cruises toward the lodge, passing alongside some moist hollows where the trees grow tall. The hike then joins the Hepatica Loop, which circles a steep wooded hill and dips to a drainage rich in wildflowers. Over twenty-five different species are purported to be along this trail. You'll get a close-up look at the Highwood Lodge before backtracking to join the Old Farm Loop.

The Old Farm Loop uses former roadbeds to get around on mostly level terrain in younger woods. The trail takes you directly to the cleared view of the Ohio River. A contemplation bench beckons. Sit down and scan into Kentucky and the waterway dividing Ohio from Kentucky, flowing 300 feet lower in elevation from where you stand. The path continues meandering through former farm coun-try mixed with some older woods. It opens onto a meadow the county is keeping cleared, part as prairie where summer flowers thrive and part as meadow for wildlife. The Old Farm Loop continues through mostly open terrain before it ends. Backtrack to the trailhead.

Miles and Directions

0.0   From the upper end of the parking area, away from the Highwood Lodge, pick up the gravel foot trail heading south, away from the lodge. Join a gravel track in deep woods with big oak and beech trees.

0.1   Reach a split. Turn right onto the Trout Lily Trail, heading westerly toward the lodge. Shortly pass an old hand-crank cistern pump, used to draw water for cattle. Today the area around it is completely wooded. Meander along a hollow with big trees.

0.4   Reach the Hepatica Loop. Stay left, descending an elaborate staircase into a hollow. Begin circling around the north side of the lodge in a wildflower-rich area. Reach another staircase and observation deck, ascending seventy-four steps behind the lodge. Emerge in the back of the building. You might want to backtrack if there is a wedding under way (after grabbing a piece of cake); otherwise, curve into the front yard and pick up the Trout Lily Trail leading back in the woods. Stay left after completing this loop.

0.9   Return to the spur trail leading left back to the parking area after backtracking on the Trout Lily Trail. Now, head straight on the Old Farm Loop.

1.0   The Old Farm Loop splits. Stay right, heading southbound for the edge of a bluff above the Ohio River.

1.2   Turn right at the spur trail to the overlook. Here, enjoy a southward view into the Bluegrass State.

1.4   Bridge a branch.

1.5   Bisect a grassy clearing where the O'Donnell Cabin once stood. Turn north beyond the clearing, shortly entering a field.

1.6   Reach a four-way junction in a field. Stay right, looping through a meadow. Watch for deer and rabbits early or late in the day.

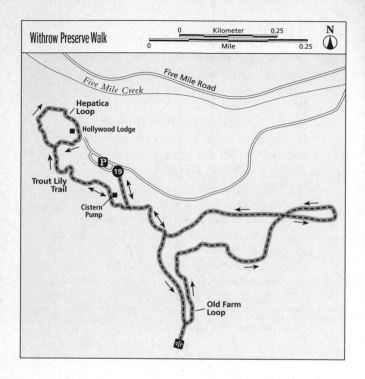

Withrow Preserve Walk

Five Mile Creek

Five Mile Road

Hepatica Loop

Hollywood Lodge

P 19

Trout Lily Trail

Cistern Pump

Old Farm Loop

N

0   Kilometer   0.25

0   Mile   0.25

1.8 Finish the mini-loop. Keep straight, continuing westerly.

2.1 Complete the Old Farm Loop. Backtrack toward the trail-head.

2.3 Reach the trailhead, completing the hike.

20 California Woods Nature Preserve

This 110-acre nature preserve contains not one but two designated National Recreation Trails that you can hike. The California Junction Trail traces an old railroad bed, while the Trillium Valley Trail explores a wildflower-laden hillside above Lick Run Creek. Your loop also explores various forest types and even visits a meadow where prairie flowers thrive. The hike does have many hills yet can be walked by just about everyone.

Distance: 2.8-mile loop
Approximate hiking time: 2.0 to 3.0 hours
Difficulty: Moderate, has several hills
Trail surface: Natural surfaces
Best season: Year-round
Other trail users: None
Canine compatibility: No dogs permitted

Fees and permits: No fees or permits required
Schedule: Sunrise to sunset
Maps: California Woods Nature Preserve; USGS Newport
Trail contacts: Cincinnati Parks, 950 Eden Park Dr., Cincinnati, OH 45202; (513) 352-4080; www.cincyparks.com

Finding the trailhead: From exit 72 on I-275 east of downtown Cincinnati, take US 52 west, Kellogg Avenue, passing the Cincinnati Waterworks, traveling a total of 1.0 mile from the interstate, then turn right into the preserve. Watch out as this right turn is at the bottom of a hill as Kellogg Avenue is curving left. Enter the preserve, traveling 0.3 mile on a very narrow road to reach the nature center. If the road is gated before you reach the nature center, park there at the lot where the gate crosses the park road. GPS: N39° 4' 39.11", W84° 25' 1.44"

The Hike

This heavily wooded preserve is an oasis of greenery through which travel several trails. Also, a very narrow paved road bisects the park. This narrow paved road is used as a trail connector for this hike and for most other hikes that people go on here, so be careful when you drive it and keep an ear and eye out for cars while you are walking on it. The hike comprises numerous different nature trails, and you can add or subtract any of them to adjust your hike. Having an extensive trail network gives you the flexibility to try different trails on subsequent visits.

This hike leaves the nature center west on the park road to reach the California Junction Trail, which rises under beech, buckeye, and tulip trees to meet the historic railroad grade. Follow it before dropping off the hill to rejoin the railroad grade, climbing gently as the old railroad right-of-way makes a lumbering 180-degree turn. Trains can climb and turn at limited grades. If the climb is too steep or the turn too sharp, the railroads can't negotiate them; therefore, when laying out the track, engineers end up with gentle grades and moderate turns.

The Trillium Valley Trail is much narrower, sneaking its way up a tight drainage where trilliums, Solomon's seal, and other wildflowers thrive. This and other hollows that you will be curving in and out of are moist and north-facing, making them ideal for blooms. Later, you will descend back to Lick Run Creek, where gravel bars and exposed limestone add geological beauty. The Meadow Trail, with its clearings, adds yet another dimension to the hike. The Ridge Trail takes you on hilltops before returning to Lick Run Creek for the final time.

Miles and Directions

0.0 From the parking area at the nature center, walk west on the park road back toward the entrance.

0.1 Turn right onto the California Junction Trail after passing the Trillium Valley Trail. The slender path climbs steeply to a ridge. The California Junction Trail splits when it meets the railbed of the old Cincinnati-Portsmouth Railroad. Turn right here, northbound.

0.4 Turn left, away from the old railbed. The footing becomes irregular as you walk through pawpaw and tulip trees. Descend wood steps.

0.5 Rejoin the railbed of the Cincinnati-Portsmouth Railroad. Turn south. The floodplain of the Little Miami River is visible to your right. Cross bridges spanning streamlets flowing off the hillside to your left. Note the berms the railbed cuts through. Imagine a train traveling where you are walking. You may even see bits of coal at your feet.

1.1 Finish the loop of the California Junction Trail. Descend back to the park road and turn left back toward the nature center.

1.3 Turn left onto the Trillium Valley Trail, beginning a solid ascent. Cross over a couple of small hollows and keep climbing.

1.5 A spur trail leads left to an oddly shaped double sycamore trunk. Reach a trail junction downhill from here. Stay left with the Moon Ridge Trail as the Ravine Trail goes right.

1.8 Reach another trail junction. Stay left with the Moon Ridge Trail as the Beech Trail descends right. Bridge a tributary that will offer cascades when running.

1.9 Stay left at the next trail junction, now on the Upper Thicket Trail.

2.1 Rock hop Lick Run Creek, joining a gravel bar near a limestone bluff. Just ahead, emerge on the park road. Head right on the road, then reach a small loop in the road. Meet the Meadow Trail at the top of the loop road as it heads south.

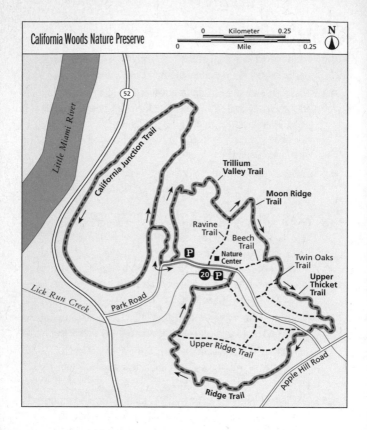

California Woods Nature Preserve

0   Kilometer   0.25

0   Mile   0.25

N

Little Miami River

California Junction Trail

52

Trillium
Valley Trail

Moon Ridge
Trail

Ravine
Trail

Beech
Trail

Nature
Center

Twin Oaks
Trail

Upper
Thicket
Trail

Lick Run Creek

Park Road

20

Upper Ridge Trail

Ridge Trail

Apple Hill Road

2.3   Pass through a clearing with multiple paths that join together on the lower end of the clearing.

2.5   Meet the Ridge Trail. Stay right, as a user-created path descends from the hill left. Just ahead the trail splits again. Stay left with the Ridge Trail as the Upper Ridge Trail keeps right.

2.8   Reach a field after descending. Cross the field, bridge Lick Creek, and complete the hike.

About the Author

Johnny Molloy is a writer and adventurer with an economics degree from the University of Tennessee. He has become skilled in a variety of outdoor environments and written over three dozen books, including hiking, camping, paddling, and comprehensive regional guidebooks as well as true outdoor adventure books. Molloy, a member of the American Hiking Society, has also written numerous articles for magazines, websites, and blogs. He resides in Johnson City, Tennessee, but spends his winters in Florida. For the latest on Molloy's pursuits and work, please visit www.johnnymolloy.com.

What's So Special about Unspoiled, Natural Places?

Beauty Solitude Wildness Freedom Quiet Adventure
Serenity Inspiration Wonder Excitement
Relaxation   Challenge

There's a lot to love about our treasured public lands, and the reasons are different for each of us. Whatever your reasons are, the national **Leave No Trace** education program will help you discover special outdoor places, enjoy them, and preserve them—today and for those who follow. By practicing and passing along these simple principles, you can help protect the special places you love from being loved to death.

The Principles of **Leave No Trace**

- Plan ahead and prepare
- Travel and camp on durable surfaces
- Dispose of waste properly
- Leave what you find
- Minimize campfire impacts
- Respect wildlife
- Be considerate of other visitors

Leave No Trace is a national nonprofit organization dedicated to teaching responsible outdoor recreation skills and ethics to everyone who enjoys spending time outdoors.

To learn more or to become a member, please visit us at www.LNT.org or call (800) 332-4100.

Leave No Trace, P.O. Box 997, Boulder, CO 80306

AMERICAN HIKING SOCIETY

Because you

hike.

We're with you
every step of the way

American Hiking Society gives voice to the more than 75 million Americans who hike and is the only national organization that promotes and protects foot trails, the natural areas that surround them, and the hiking experience. Our work is inspiring and challenging, and is built on three pillars:

Volunteerism and Stewardship

We organize and coordinate nationally recognized programs—including Volunteer Vacations, National Trails Day ®, and the National Trails Fund—that help keep our trails open, safe, and enjoyable.

Policy and Advocacy

We work with Congress and federal agencies to ensure funding for trails, the preservation of natural areas, and the protection of the hiking experience.

Outreach and Education

We expand and support the national constituency of hikers through outreach and education as well as partnerships with other recreation and conservation organizations.

Join us in our efforts. Become an American Hiking Society member today!

American Hiking Society

1422 Fenwick Lane · Silver Spring, MD 20910 · (800) 972-8608
www.AmericanHiking.org · info@AmericanHiking.org

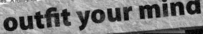